THEN AND NOW. HE'S NOT DONE WITH ME YET!

His first twenty five years. A young man's struggle for success. Memories of childhood education, aspirations, identity crisis, family dysfunction, child abuse, alcohol abuse, love, sex, rape, violence, and discrimination.

An inspirational story about a Latino American reaching for his future.

By William Mon T.

Copyright © 2014 by William Montoya

Printed in USA by Greater Is He Publishing

Editor and Interior Designer: Tony Bradford

Front Cover Designer: Dionne Preston

Back Cover Designer: Robert King

All rights reserved. No part of this book may be reproduced or transmitted in any form or by any means without written permission from the author.

ISBN: 978-1-938950-42-1

Greater Is He Publishing
9824 E. Washington St.
Chagrin Falls, Ohio 44023
Phone: 216.288.9315
www.GreaterIsHePublishing.com

CONTENTS

Preface	1
Chapter 1: Where It Began	3
Chapter 2: La Familia	15
Chapter 3: The Dream	19
Chapter 4: Public to Private	30
Chapter 5: Sex	42
Chapter 6: Scotland	53
Chapter 7: High School	63
Chapter 8: All At Once	76
Chapter 9: Why Me?	93
Chapter 10: "Nothing Comes to Sleepers, But a Dream"	106
Chapter 11: The Last Summer	111
Chapter 12: College Freshmen	123
Chapter 13: Academics	136
Chapter 14: Sophomore Year	147
Chapter 15: Jerome	157
Chapter 16: Junior Year	162
Chapter 17: Returning Home	188
Chapter 18: Caren	193
Chapter 19: Last Year	204

Chapter 20: Student Teaching	211
Chapter 21: Alpha	222
Chapter 22: My Kids	226
Chapter 23: Acceptance	229
Chapter 24: My House	234
Chapter 25: A Good Year?	240
Chapter 26: I Was Really Thinking About It!	243
Chapter 27: The End of the First Quarter	258

To my mom, tú eres la inspiración de mi vida.

To Diego, I am where I am, I am who I am, because of you. Thank You.

To my sisters.

To my father.

To Jason.

To my Sands.

To Garry, A'maya, and Antoinette. Papi loves you so much for the joy and love you fill my heart with!

To all of my kids (students). You are the reason I get up in the morning.

To my friends, you have accepted me for me, which is the biggest gift you can ever give me.

To my pastor for giving me the courage to take this memoir out of an old box and begin to heal.

I love you all.

Los amo.

Preface

It seems like every time I go through something major, I have this dream I used to have when I was kid. The interesting part about the dream is that although it was a very long time ago, I manage to add and subtract different characters from the past and the present while having the dream.

I don't know if you would call this autobiography; I've only been on Earth for twenty five years. I guess you can just say this is sort of a recap of my life as I remember it.

I have been through a lot. I have gone through stuff that most people probably could not handle very well. To tell you the absolute truth, I have trouble accepting some of the things I've done and experienced. By no means am I saying that I'm special; I'm sure there is someone out there who probably has been through a lot more than me.

My stories and memories are not meant to boast, not at all! I'm just someone who has made it through a difficult stage of life. I hope this "Spilling of Guts" allows someone who is going through rough times to be inspired, to go on fighting. I know it's easier said than done. I want to share my struggles so that folks, especially young Latino and

Black adults like me, can see that success is not a state of being but simply a peaceful state of mind.

I studied to be a teacher not solely to teach academics, but to educate young minds about life. My experiences as an educator have allowed me to help young people work through difficult times. Maybe I can inspire one young mind to overcome hindrances, family dysfunction, abuse or something which seems to be unconquerable, impossible to handle, and/or incurable. I have discovered the role given to me by the almighty is to be here to listen, advise, guide, or simply be there for young people who come into my life. If I am the cause of a smile, I have done my job. If I am the cause of someone working harder, I have received an extra bonus. If I am the cause of someone going off to college, I am in my glory. My vocation has then been successful. That is God's role for me. I accept it.

I am the first to admit I'm not where I want to be financially, professionally, even socially, but I am not ungrateful. I thank God for all he has given me and hope there are even better times in store for me.

Chapter 1
WHERE IT BEGAN

Is it possible I can wake up and remember a dream I once had as a kid? My God, what a spooky feeling. The weirdest part was, as I was dreaming, my brain was saying, "This is an old dream." I actually knew I was having an old dream as I was dreaming. It was a dream I began having when I was about ten years old. This dream has caused me to remember, recall, relive, rethink, review, rekindle, and return to my life as I have lived it for a quarter century.

At the time, I was in the fifth grade attending Case Elementary School. It was my first Cleveland Public School. My teacher's name was Mrs. Jones. My best friend was Tyrone, Tyrone Frazier. Tyrone was Black. For me, this was so different. It was then when odd things started to happen. When I say odd things, I mean on the outside as well as on the inside. Knowing my life, my world, and who I was began right here. Tyrone was one of my first odd situations.

Mom and my father moved the family to Cleveland

from a small town in Connecticut. Most of my friends as a child were White. The neighborhoods I grew up in were White for the most part. I am not saying I only had White friends. Although I had contact with Blacks, I never really knew any Blacks until I met Tyrone.

The horror stories we heard about inner city schools had frightened me so much. The kids in the neighborhood told my sister and me the schools in Cleveland were really rowdy and extremely bad. I was terrified about going to school in a big city. Tyrone was very nice to me on the first day of school, Thank God!

Tyrone

Tyrone was the only light in my life at the time. In September, he was the only one who made me feel a little better. The kids on the street really didn't bother to get to know us the summer we moved to Cleveland. One day, I tried to introduce myself, but they brushed me off. I never tried making friends again. Tyrone was different. He was tall and slim with an afro. Afros and Jerry curls were the "in" hairstyles. He always had a pick in his hair or in his back pocket. His appearance was deceiving since he looked way older than ten years old. He was just a tall kid, a lot taller than me and very athletic. I sure was jealous of

Tyrone, but not in a bad way.

Out of all the boys in Mrs. Jones' class, Tyrone was the most athletic. In gym class, he was the fastest and the strongest. Every time we played a game, everyone wanted Tyrone on their team. Physique was very important in the fifth grade. I remember the boys talking in the bathroom about who had the biggest muscles. Tyrone always made the rest of the boys feel inferior. He wasn't thin and he wasn't fat; he just had more muscles than any of the boys. His chest and arms were well defined. He'd show off his pecs when we'd get ready for gym class. He'd boast about his biceps being like rocks and his six pack stomach. I knew what rocks were, but it wasn't until years later when I found out what a six pack was. Tyrone's biceps *were* like rocks. When he made a muscle, his biceps would rise like a balloon. Although I considered him my best friend, I still couldn't help but to feel a little jealous of his physique, especially his muscles; his chest, stomach, and of course his rock-like biceps. I used to go home and do pushups and chin ups on the swing set in the park. Tyrone told me that was the way to get big muscles. I wanted to be just like Tyrone. I wanted to be as popular as he was in class and in gym. Even at recess when the rest of the classes were out on the playground, everyone wanted him to be on their side for football and kick ball. I felt lucky to be Tyrone's friend.

As the days went by and the "new kid" syndrome wore off, I met some of Tyrone's other friends. One of them was Aaron. When I first meet him, I felt something was wrong. The tension was thick enough to cut. I sensed Aaron was feeling sad, even angry, at how close Tyrone and I had become. I later learned Aaron and Tyrone were best friends before I came to Cleveland. It was during lunch when I first knew there was something bothering Aaron. Tyrone would invite me to sit next to him, and I could tell Aaron did not like it. I didn't want to start any trouble, so I tried to make other friends. I found myself in a bind because while I was trying to avoid a problem with Aaron, Tyrone thought I did not want to be his friend anymore. After I told him how I felt, he told me I was silly for thinking that way about Aaron. But I knew better; I knew Aaron had a problem with our friendship, I wasn't stupid. I didn't want any problems. It was tough enough dealing with the new school, neighborhood, city, and friends. Not to mention the changes my family was going through, especially with Mom and my father. I didn't want any more drama in my life. Fortunately, later, Aaron, Tyrone, and I, became the best of friends.

I was dealing with lots of things at the time. I remember feeling comfortable enough with Tyrone that I could tell him anything. I could talk to him about the things that bothered me. At times, I cried in front of him. That was difficult, even embarrassing, for me because at that age it wasn't cool to cry. But sometimes the pressure would just get the best of me. I'd start to tell a story and end up mad and in tears. Tyrone was different because he listened. I could cry or be angry around him and he didn't laugh or make fun of me. I was having a hard time accepting the changes with Mom, my father, and especially my new home.

Cleveland, Ohio was.... WOW! Compared to Norwalk, it was like living in New York City. Looking back, moving to a big city was an overwhelming feeling for the whole family. I don't think we were prepared to go from little to big so quickly. In Norwalk, I felt like I knew everyone by name, the people in the neighborhood and all the kids at school. Cleveland was the complete opposite. I felt like a number. I remember the oohs and the aahhs we made coming off the highway, and driving into the city, because of the skyscrapers and all the people we saw. The thing that stuck out the most was all the Black people. My mom looked at my father, and even though they did not say anything, I could tell what they were thinking. I remember thinking it was going to be interesting how well our little family would adapt to a big city. There was a huge difference between Norwalk, Connecticut and Cleveland, Ohio.

A BIG difference!

Our family was used to feeling unique. It seemed everywhere we went, whether it was church or going to school, we were the only Latinos or of the few that knew two languages. My first impression and feelings about the area where my father rented our apartment was similar to the way I felt in school back in Norwalk. I was the only Latino student among all the White kids. Only now, in Cleveland, I was the only Latino among all Black kids. I remember wondering if any Whites or Latinos lived on my block. It seemed like everyone around me was Black.

Mom and my father are both Colombian, and although we lived in the states, we were raised as proud Latinos. We ate Spanish cooking, spoke Spanish in the home, and practiced Colombian traditions and customs. Some of those customs included discipline...the old fashioned Latino way. I'll go more into detail later on.

My mom wore the pants in the family. She paid the bills

and dealt with all the financial things of the family. My father just worked. He worked two jobs in Norwalk. We barely saw him. He got up before we went to school and by the time we arrived from school, he was on his way out to his second job. The big thing in my family was money…always money. For as long as I can remember, money was always the topic of discussion. I remember the fights about money or the lack of money. My father would say he worked to the bone and never had the chance to enjoy his money. Mom, well, Mom insisted he give her his pay. She would pay the bills and take care of whatever was needed concerning us and the house. I really shouldn't say house because we rented until 1981. The majority of the fights concerned the rent and how expensive it was to live in Norwalk. That's when the whole idea about moving away started.

Leaving

My father and his friend took a trip to Cleveland for fun; that's when he convinced my father it was a good place to move the family. I remember him telling Mom the rent in Cleveland was a third of what they were paying in Norwalk. Mom told him if he found a job in Cleveland and a place for the family she would move. And my father did just that very thing. The last summer we spent in Norwalk, my father left for about a month, and when he returned, we were told to start packing. We left within a week of his return from Cleveland.

What a difference with Mom when we arrived at the new house. She just began to cry. She was infuriated my father would bring us to a house that was half the size of the house in Norwalk and ten times as bad. It was an apartment on the main avenue which connected the neighborhood with downtown Cleveland. There was no yard, the house was ugly, and the apartment was dirty, smelly and it was infested with mice and roaches. It was then that I remember more problems with Mom and my father and more problems with me. Mom had her hopes up real high about moving. How could she not? My father had made Cleveland out to be the best thing since buttered bread. Boy, was Mom disappointed and let down. Cleveland was obviously not at all what she had anticipated it to be.

Since I can remember, I have always been the one to feel everything; the problems that Mom and my father were having and all the tragedies we went through. My older sister, Gladys, and my younger sister, Alina, really did not seem to pay attention to the problems. Maybe they did, but it seemed to me I was the only one worrying about the things that were happening. Now that I think about it, I wonder if the girls felt the problems in the household as much as I did. It didn't seem like it.

That summer, I spent most of the time writing everyone in Norwalk. After a while, they stopped writing, and so did I. I realized this was going to be my new home. It was a very cold and sad feeling.

Cheaper Meant More Costly

Mom and my father became worse. Not a day went by that Mom didn't remind my father how miserable she felt living like a poor woman. She hated the city life, but most of all she despised the fact we were living at a lower level than we had ever lived. Mom had to get a job in order to dress us. I remember Mom telling us she would go hungry before she saw her kids go to school looking like "gamines." (Gamines are the orphans that run the streets in Colombia). We were raised with pride. Proud of being Latino and proud to be in the United States, Mom made sure we looked clean and well-dressed in public. There was no way Mom would let us look shabby or poor. Accepting clothes from other people was forbidden, and asking to wear other people's clothes was out of the question. Mom did not want us to feel poor, but we did. It was a proud feeling in a way. We had everything we needed, but it was never too expensive nor to fancy. Mom remembered the gamines from her childhood, and she always made sure to tell us we were not gamines. Although the cost of living *was* cheaper, it robbed the family of our peace in the home. Living cheaper ended up costing us our happiness as a family. I don't think my father really thought things through. Sure, the cost of living was less expensive, but I don't think my father realized the wages in Cleveland were way lower than what he was making in Norwalk.

My Mom

Mom left my father in Colombia when my oldest sister, Gladys, was six years old. My father lost an eye at a construction site and could not find any work to support Gladys and Mom. From what I understand, Mom was the attending nurse the day they brought in my father. He apparently had stuck a metal rod in his eye. Mom fell in love with him, and later they married. At the time, Mom was twenty-nine, and my father was twenty. I do not understand the whole story, but I do know that Mom gave birth to Gladys at thirty and me at thirty-five.

Around October of '69, Mom saved up enough to leave Colombia. She was pregnant with me when she came to the U.S.A. She was greeted by my father's sisters who lived in New York City. The story as told to me by Mom was they treated her poorly. She described herself as a Cinderella. She cleaned, did their laundry, cooked and babysat all of my cousins. In short, Mom wasn't happy and made certain we understood how she felt about her sisters in law. On a happier note, she did tell me that my aunt's husband, who is also my Godfather, treated her very kindly. He would slide her money on the low and sometimes went out and bought me things. She described him as my foster dad for the first three years of my life. I always wanted to meet him but never got the chance until years later. Mom said he treated me like one of his own. If it had not been for his moral and financial support, the times would have been harder for her and for me. I wanted to meet him so I could tell him, "Thank You!"

I imagine how difficult it was being in a foreign country. Mom did not know or speak any English, but she managed by pointing and drawing pictures on a little note pad. I envision this very determined, dedicated, and hardworking mother, and it makes me feel so proud I am her son. I admire my mom for all she has been through and what she is going through. I think that is who I picked up my fighting spirit from, my mom.

Mom moved to Norwalk when I was two. She worked all day to save up enough money to send for my father and Gladys. She worked at a factory making shades. I can't begin to imagine how it must have been for her to go from being a nurse to working in a factory. Mom says she worked with love and gratitude. Love for her new home, the USA, and grateful she had her health and her son's health. My father and Gladys arrived when I was going on three years old.

Chapter 2
LA FAMILIA

Gladys and I did not get along whatsoever. I can remember how she used to make me feel. I recall lots of teasing and feeling very angry even to the point where I felt a loss of control. My father always sided with her over things, and I always got the whippings when we'd get into a quarrel.

My father was very strong with me. I cannot remember any warmth or closeness as a child from him. He drank a lot when I was kid. That, I do remember...Clearly! I remember the times he would come home intoxicated. Mom and I would end up cleaning his vomit. We were not allowed to talk to my father or be around him when he was drunk. He was very brutal and at times very violent. He used to smoke too until Mom put his clothes out on the porch and insisted either he go or the cigarettes go. I remember he just stopped. He quit just like that. But he did not stop drinking. My father loved to drink "agua ardiente" (burning water). I guess in

Colombia, my father drank every day. Maybe this was THE reason Mom ventured to the U.S. Maybe losing his eye and not being able to support his family affected him more than what anyone thought. He lost his wife and missed out on a son for three years. It must have been really difficult for him to watch his wife support the family. I'm sure it wasn't easy for his proud, Latino ego to accept.

Having a family was very different for me. I had to get used to a sister whom I did not get along with, and a father who took sides with her over every little dispute. My father was scary. He had a very bad temper. As a kid, the worse thing Mom could tell me was, "Wait until your father gets home." My father worked all day and was very tired all the time. He did not want to hear about his son misbehaving at school or at home. There were times when Mom would get really angry with us and would threaten us with him. There were times we thought she meant it; informing him of some sort of misbehavior we committed. Those were the hardest moments. We would plead with her not to say anything to him. I recall one time locating a belt out of the closet and begged Mom to hit me herself. There was no reasoning with my father. The consequences for acting like a fool in school or at home were brutal.

He became an instant Dr. Jekyll and Mr. Hyde. I remember feeling like hell all of those times I had to sit on the bed waiting for him to enter the room to whip me. I felt like my insides were going to explode. I remember how it felt to wait in the room butt -naked. Waiting for him to come in with a belt wrapped around his wrist and hand was agonizing. It was easier to deal with beatings when they occurred on the spur of the moment, no waiting, just...boom... and it was over. Like the time we were at Caldor's, a department store in Norwalk.

I remember throwing a tantrum because I wanted a toy my father said I could not have. Without thinking, he transformed! Very energetically and angrily, he zipped off his belt and swung it around the back of his head like Zorro. The only thing I could do was wince and cry as loud as I could. My father commenced to kicking my behind in Caldor's that day. He told me being in public would not stop him from whipping my ass. We were warned never to cause him embarrassment because not only would we get it in the store, but we'd also get it in the car and at home. I say these whippings were easier to deal with because beatings like those you did not have to sit waiting, suffering, and worrying. Spontaneous beatings just happened! No time to prepare. Just quick and fast!

Beating after beating became the norm. As I was growing up, the beatings were making me hate him to the point where I would have the dream about killing him. The dream which began after the sled incident.

Chapter 3
THE DREAM

I spent an entire Norwalk winter shoveling snow and making a little money to buy a snow sled. Mom was going to buy it for me anyway, but I felt more important earning the money. I told Mom I wanted to buy it myself. The real reason was, buying it with my own money meant I did not have to share it with my younger sister, Alina.

I made sure to let my father know this was my sled and no one else's. That was where I had made the mistake. That summer, I was coming home from the YMCA when in the distance I saw a bunch of the neighborhood kids on the front steps of our house. My heart began to beat faster and faster as I got closer to our front steps. My eyes could not believe what they were seeing. I noticed Alina had my sled out. She and her friends were sliding down the cement steps of the house with the sled!

My father was prepared. It seemed to me he had it all planned. He knew I would be coming home since my

YMCA swimming lessons ran certain hours. He had a chair on the sidewalk in front of the steps. As I got closer and closer, I felt the anger in my dream rush to my head. It was as though he had put the chair there because he knew I would go off. It almost looked as if he was on guard. Without thinking, I stomped over to the top at the steps and grabbed the sled underneath Alina's legs. She fell to the ground and let out a scream. As my father ran to the top of the steps, I could see the transformation of Dr. Jekyll and Mr. Hide. The anger in his eyes and the love in his heart for the beating he would later justify to my mom, for me snatching the sled and making Alina fall; was inevitable and unavoidable. This beating resulted in a dislocated shoulder. One of many injuries I suffered at the fate of my father. My father took a hack saw from under the cement steps and chopped the sled into tiny pieces. I remember thinking it really didn't matter. The sliding down the cement steps had burned holes all over the bottom. I consoled myself by thinking, "It would have never slid down the snow covered hills like before anyway." I did however remain upset and very angry at Alina and my father.

As a boy, it felt like any chance he got to beat me he would take in a flash. The beatings made Mom and him fight. She would protect me as much as she could. My father nevertheless found excuses for beating me up. After all, he had to explain the bruises when Mom got home from work. He was a master at justifying my beatings.

Alina entered my life in 1975. Alina is the youngest. Needless to say, she was my father's new little girl. She picked up where Gladys had left off. My father also took her side on everything just as he did with Gladys. There was greater hostility between my father and I after Alina was born. My father adored her. He gave her anything she wanted, anything she cried for. All she had to do was get into his arms. She got anything she wanted even if it belonged to me. This was evident with the sled. What really angered me the most was that Alina knew she could get what she wanted even if it meant that *I* would be hurt physically or mentally. My father was not only a master at beating me, but he was a pro at making me feel like I was nothing. I actually preferred to be beat rather than to be called names and made fun of. My father knew that calling me names hurt me more than anything. To me it felt like Alina never cared about anyone else's feelings but her own. She simply wanted things her way. I honestly can say I never felt any sibling warmth for my sisters during these years. The only time I felt any real concern for one of them was the day Gladys dropped Alina.

Gladys was carrying Alina on a public bus, and as we got off the bus, Gladys lost her balance, and the next thing you know Alina was unconscious on the pavement. I remember thinking if she died I would still have to deal with Gladys. I know that was a terrible thought, but I could not take the attention the girls received. It made me feel transparent. It is amazing how I can remember those feelings when they were so long ago and still remember the emotions. As I write all this, I relive the frustration and anger. I lived with such hate day in and day out that I can't believe I mended those bridges and have a relationship with my sisters today. Alina was fine after the fall. She didn't need medical attention, although I think her fall affected her. A couple of years after the sled incident and the dislocated shoulder, we moved into an apartment in the Norwalk projects. Our apartment number was J12. I'll never forget it! We even had our own parking space with J12 written in the pavement. I remember fighting with the other kids to stay off of the parking space even though we were not supposed to be near the parking spaces. My father made it clear to stay away from the lot and cars. We weren't supposed to play there because they were on a hill; the hill turned like a corkscrew and it was dangerous since the cars were always coming in and out in a circle.

    I remember one summer when some of the bigger kids were roller skating down the winding hill. One was killed. A car coming up the hill hit the boy as he was going down and around one of the bends. Now, I am realizing as an adult and as a teacher that children like to be told not to do things. It makes them feel challenged. They want to do it even more when they are told not to do it. A neighbor once told my mom she had to stop being our "watch tower." He said to her, "Children will do what you tell them not to do just for the sake of the challenge of getting away with it." And you know, that man was right; I went down that forbidden winding hill one day. I was dared to do so by the kids in the projects. I headed down the hill on my bike. Just as I was reaching the bottom, a car came around the last bend (it was the car's first bend if you really think about it). I went into pure shock. My natural reaction was to hit the brakes. I slammed on the brakes, and my bike threw me, head first. I landed into some loose gravel. I remember a lady picking me up off the ground and putting a rag on my bleeding forehead. I thought I was going to die. The pain was unbearable. All I could remember was yelling, "J12, J1 2, J12," over and over again. The lady must have known I was screaming the number of the apartment because she took me straight to my building. All the while, I was walking up the hill toward our apartment building, I remember thinking, "I'd better pretend the pain is so bad that my father might feel sorry for me." I knew if my father found out what really happened, he'd hit me for disobeying the rule about the hill. Thank God he was not home! When Mom saw me, she started screaming and yelling. I chuckle a little because by the time I had reached the front steps of the apartment building, I was calm. But after Mom saw all the blood, she went off screaming and yelling, which in turn made me go off all over again. Most of it was just because I wanted attention. She put my head in the sink and ran the water over my bleeding forehead. She kept on saying "¿Vuelve?, ¿Vuelve?" meaning, "Will you disobey again? Will you disobey again?" This is an expression that means did you learn a lesson? Mom cleaned me up as best as she could and told me not to let my father see my head. She combed my hair forward to cover the cut marks across my head. You know, come to think of it, he never knew; or better yet, I don't think he ever knew what happened that day. But maybe he did.

My father was the type that did not care about you being in pain due to your own stupidity, disobedience, or negligence. We were told that if we ever got hurt or if the oldest let the youngest get hurt, we would all get a butt whipping. I never understood why he was like that. But here again, now that I am an adult, I know why; family is supposed to watch over each other.

Name Calling

We had moved out of the projects when I was in the third grade and into a two family house in South Norwalk. I was bussed to a bilingual school, Broadriver Elementary. I was going to this school for Spanish. At home we spoke Spanish, but in school everything was in English. I started having trouble with the work, so Mom signed me up for the bilingual program. I learned how to read, write and speak proper Spanish at Broadriver. I had other classes in English like the other schools but there was always someone who spoke Spanish just in case I needed help understanding something. I learned what it was to be Latino, and I can remember a lot of pride was instilled in me by the staff and parents. The only thing about Broadriver that I hated was the teasing, Jose, and his friends. They were bullies. I still remember feeling so alone and helpless. It was awful! There were so many bullies in school and on the bus ride to and from school. Everyday I'd come home crying because someone was messing with me, hitting me, taking something from me, or just teasing me about something. My father was home one of those days I got off the bus crying. For a long time, I continuously complained about a bully named Jose. My father had had it! He told me I'd better not ever get off the bus crying again. But the very next day, I got off the bus crying because Jose struck me in the back of my head as I was getting off the bus. I figured there was no way my father would be home two days in a row. I could cry for Mom, and she would feel sorry for me and comfort me with some ice cream or candy. Boy was wrong! When I opened the door, there he was waiting. It was too late to pull myself together. My father grabbed me by an arm and dragged me to the car. He followed the school bus until Jose got off. He sure did. He stopped the car and demanded I get out and fight Jose on his front lawn. I didn't argue with my father. At that point I was so scared and so full of adrenalin, I felt myself transforming into another person. Just as I saw my father turn into Dr. Jekyll and Mr. Hide in my dream, so did I. I ran up to Jose and tackled him to the ground. In a moment of rage I began to pound him with my closed fists and kick him with all my might. I screamed at him, "I am sick of you, I am sick of you." The kids on the bus watched the whole thing. I remember their cheers through the bus windows. I remember feeling and saying to myself, "This is it, I've got to show them, all of them!" I had to show everyone I was not going to be messed with anymore. My father told me never to come home beat up again, because if I did, he would kick my ass for 1, getting into a fight, and 2, for getting into a fight and losing it. The kids at Broadriver Elementary did not mess with me as much after that day. The dream had gotten worse after my fight with Jose. The dream where I stab my father to his death.

 The dream would occur on the nights I'd lay awake being angry at all the teasing and name calling I had endured during the day. Most of the teasing was about being a sissy, or acting like a girl, or being around the girls all the time. I realize now that I must have given the children reasons to make fun of me. Maybe it was the way I carried myself. But it wasn't just the children. I can remember overhearing the gym teacher telling my homeroom teacher I ran like a girl and screamed like a girl. Needless to say, I was devastated. I remember being called gay, a faggot, "maricon" and other horrible names. It hurt like hell, but I would pretend it didn't. Until it was time for bed as I'd lay there and brew and think, and think and brew.

People have said to me as an adult that I have many feminine characteristics. I realize and accept this now as an adult but with a grain of salt. I have come to realize I have been this way all my life. As a child, I guess I was not aware of the way I carried myself. As an adult, I now am very aware at all times of how I carry myself and how I may come across to people. I find myself studying how men, in general, carry themselves. I try to copycat, imitate their movements, the way they walk, use their hands, stand, things like that. Since I have accepted the fact I do have feminine qualities, I do my best to try and conceal or change them. They may have come from having sisters and no brothers. Maybe they came from having all female friends. Maybe it was growing up with pretty colors, hair ribbons, and baby dolls. Maybe it was because I didn't have someone to play football, baseball, or wrestle with. You know, all the "boy" sports. Maybe I was born this way. The "maybees" drove me crazy, absolutely crazy. The maybees that began to torture me at night.

I did not care to spend the rest of my life being called

names or having people whisper things behind my back. I know I wasn't supposed to care what other people felt or said about me, and today I don't to a certain extent, but I'm only human. Sometimes, I just wanted to feel accepted, especially when being introduced to new people.

It was not until after I met Tyrone that he was incorporated in the dream. His face vague, not clear, but I know it's him helping me up after stabbing my father. In the dream, Tyrone makes me feel relieved and consoled. Tyrone lifts me, putting his arm under my arm. He lifts me up off the floor, takes his hands and wipes my face, cleaning away the tears and rage. He says, "Let's get out of here; he can't bother you no more." I look into his eyes, embrace him and walk away. That's when I wake up. There have been times when I try to make the dream last a little longer, but I wake up. I understand that I am dreaming, and interestingly, I know that I am struggling to continue the dream but it just ends.

Why did this dream come back? I have not had a fight with my father in a long time. I have not even thought about Tyrone. I had this dream way before I met Tyrone. Why was Tyrone in the dream? What is it about this dream that makes me uneasy?

Chapter 4
PUBLIC TO PRIVATE

Mom could not take it anymore. We had become so different after moving to Cleveland. She'd tell us we sounded like street thugs. I guess she was referring to the street accent we picked up in public school. Mom did not like it at all. She would remind us that there was no need to talk incorrectly just to fit in. But there was. I used to be so aware of my grammar until the Cleveland Public Schools came into my life. It was then Mom sent us to Catholic school. Gladys went to the horrid public junior high, Willson. Alina and I went to Immaculate Conception Catholic School (The Mac). She was going into the first grade, and I was going into the sixth.

I discovered myself at "The Mac." By this I mean I began to think more about things; my feelings, ideas, and opinions. We were taught to think like masters. It was very competitive at The Mac. Boy, was it different from public school. At Case, a person was considered a brown nose or geek if they raised their hand to answer a question or participate in a class. Children were threatened to get beat up if they continued to do work and participate in class. The bullies felt they would get more work if the teacher felt everyone was learning. It was better for bullies to stay on the same subject for a long time, because it meant the work would be reviewed over and over and nothing new would be introduced. It was beyond me why children wanted to remain on the same subjects. They almost always had a gripe about new work or new lessons. I felt super frustrated at Case; I did not learn very much. Mrs. Jones was special. She gave me extra work not as a punishment but as a reward. She gave me a book to read during the summer and many puzzles to improve my spelling and writing. My last year at Case I received every major award; honor role, citizenship, math, science, attendance, behavior, merit role, spelling bee winner, and math facts champion. When Mrs. Jones found out I was going to a private school, she cried. She said I was one of her best students. I visited Mrs. Jones my sophomore year in college. She was so proud. She just kept rubbing my shoulder and repeating, "I am so proud of you." I think Mrs. Jones felt validated. That made me feel good.

The Mac was a totally different world. As for my habits, it was too late. It was hard speaking grammatically correct. Sister Stella Marie always corrected me in front of the class. The biggest problem was how to use the verb "be." It was difficult not to say, "I be, he be, she be, they be." It became so natural, so inborn in public school. Case really had an impression on my grammar. A fellow classmate at the Mac once asked me why did I act Black. And once again, I discovered how people viewed me. I could not tell I was "acting Black", nor could I tell my talk was that of the Black culture. But what was "acting Black"? What did the kids at the Mac mean when they said I sounded Black? What did acting Black mean? What did it mean when I was told I sounded like the kids at Case?

Most of the kids at Case were Black and lived in the ghetto or "The Hood," and most were very poor. At Mac, the kids were different. They seemed more in tune with school, schoolwork, grades, and obedience. They did not tolerate any wrong doing at the Mac. Believe me when I tell you they'd call home even if you looked at a teacher the wrong way. At Case, the kids talked back to the teachers. They even swore at them, and some even attacked the teachers. The Mac was a totally different world. The kids at the Mac seemed like they lived well and never worried about anything, including tuition or money. This may not have been the case, but that's the impression I had.

What made me feel different from the children was being so aware of my family's financial problems. It affected me at the Mac especially on occasions when I had to pay for fundraiser candy I could not sell or when it was time to buy new uniforms. It was a concern and a headache for my parents. I was very aware of the sacrifices being made to send me to a private school. I think this was when I began to ask less for toys and things. It became harder and harder, especially when my peers had things I knew my mom and father could never afford to give us.

Mom was paying for the Mac by working at the May Company Department Store. She started out wrapping gifts at Christmas. They kept her on after the season and moved her to the food court. Later that year, she ran the food stand and was made manager. I would catch the public bus to downtown and head right to the food stand. I was so proud of my mom. Her English improved more and more. She even went as far as to apply at Community College. She was so proud. I remember when she'd come home and ask us to help her with her homework. It was a weird feeling to help

Mom with her work because we were always used to her helping us. I thought to myself, this is what growing up was all about. The changing of roles within the family.

The Mac for me was awful as far as academics were concerned. There was so much work. The worst part was the reading assignments. I hated reading with a passion. I was never a good reader. I always found myself reading things over and over again. I could never grasp the meaning the first time. I would read my textbooks three or four times before I began to understand a concept. It felt like I was the only one in the class having a learning problem. I realized my study habits had been shot to hell at Case. Even though the teachers at the Mac pushed me, it was very difficult to get back on track with good study habits and self-discipline. I was reminded on a daily basis about the tuition and the sacrifices being made to send "my ass" to a private school. Those conversations with my parents, especially my father, lasted two seconds. My father would talk about how tired he was of working night and day and the only way I repaid him was with bad grades. And what were bad grades? Well, let's put it like this; one time, I brought home an almost perfect report card. I earned, yes *earned*, all A's except for a damned B in Reading. My father looked at the report card and said, "I am not working myself to death for you to bring home B's." What a shock that was for me! I was expecting praise for a great report card, and the topic of conversation was the damned B in reading. As I remember those times, I realize now my father's intentions were not to be an S.O.B. He did not want us to settle for anything less than what we were capable of doing. If he'd only sat down and expressed those feelings, I think my relationship with him would have been easier to deal with. I will never make that mistake if I ever have children. They will be told why things are said and why things must be done a certain way even though it may not be as pleasurable as one would like it to be.

    Mom and my father could only afford three years at the Mac, sixth, seventh, and eighth grade. I graduated from the eighth grade and applied for an all boys school, St. Edward's High School only because everyone in my class was continuing high school in a private school. I felt I should too since everyone was doing so, even though I knew my parents would never be able to afford it. I went to St. Edward's for a total of two weeks and three days.

Back to Public

    I got into fights the entire two weeks I attended St. Edwards. The children all seemed rich and bourgeois. For the first time in my life, I found myself having very ill feelings toward White people. The things they said to me hurt me very much. I was called Nigger Lover, Wet Back, Spic, and made fun of the way I talked. During class changes, the other boys would shove me in the hallway to agitate me. All of this tension began after my first physical education class.

In gym, it seemed the attention was on me because I was the fastest and the most athletic when it came to running and playing football (Imagine feeling like a Tyrone). Even though it encouraged me to work harder, it made me very bitter. I implored my mom to let me go to public school. It was a weird feeling because as I asked to leave St. Edwards, I was terrified to go to Willson Jr. High, the public junior high school in the neighborhood better known as "The Dog House."

Ever since my sister Gladys had a bad experience at Willson, I was terrified to go there. It was tough for Gladys when we moved to Cleveland. We moved during her junior high years. Anyone who can remember junior high years knows those times are, if not the most crucial times in a person's life, sure are the most important. Gladys had to leave her friends and her boyfriend whom she liked very much back in Norwalk. She was very angry when we moved to Cleveland.

I remember when Mom first enrolled us into public school, Gladys complained about the rowdiness of the building. Later, she expressed how she had problems with a girl at Willson. Apparently, Gladys was accused of calling her a name and the girl threatened to beat her up. Back in those days, when one was threatened to get beat up, word got around pretty fast.

Gladys said she did not call her a name, but apparently the girl disliked Gladys since the moment they met. Everyone said the girl was jealous because Gladys was new and very pretty and had become the center of attention as far as the boys were concerned. Later, we discovered that this was the same girl whose friends had beaten up a young lady in the bathroom. The young lady who had gotten beat up was Puerto Rican. The story goes that all the boys were crazy about this Puerto Rican girl. This did not go over too well with the Black girls. They took this young lady into the bathroom, cut her hair, and stuck her head in the toilet.

This was the same girl who came to our apartment with a group of her friends. They managed to lure Gladys out in front of the house. The girl and her friends jumped Gladys and beat her up. Gladys's new Cleveland boyfriend and all of his family came over after they heard what happened. Later that evening, they went looking for the girl and her friends to retaliate. They did just that, and it caused more problems. Gladys had to leave Willson and go to another school. That year, Willson was known for their racial tensions between Blacks and the Whites and Blacks and Latinos. And this was the school I was supposed to go to. I can only remember thinking, "Holy Crap! I am going to get beat up every day." Gladys gave me some advice. She said, "Go to school, do your work, mind your own business, and get out of the building as fast as you can." She didn't have to tell me twice! Let me say, I ran home every day that year. In the spring, I ran on the track team for Willson. I won every race at every track meet Willson competed in. I had plenty of training running from E. 55th Street to E. 32nd Street every day after school except the days when we had track meets.

I recall the time a group of boys followed me from my last period class. They were very angry because I did not let them copy from a math test we had just taken. It was my very first fight with a Black kid, or in this case, a whole group of Black kids. I was pushed several times on the concrete. There were children all over, gladiating, cheering, and egging on the whole thing. No one would help or say, "Stop, leave him alone." The kids enjoyed watching fights. After being pushed around for five minutes, I could not stand it anymore. When the last shove caused me to scrape my knees, I remember transforming again like in the dream. I heard a voice inside my head. It was my mom's voice saying, "Don't ever start a fight. If you can walk away, do so, but if someone lays a hand on you, hit their ass right back." She told me if there was ever a fight involving more than one, to defend myself any way I could. She advised me to pick up anything that started with the letter "a"; a stick, a rock, a bottle, another person if I could lift him/her. The only thing I had were my house keys. How did it end? Let's just say the kids, after this incident, referred to me as Zorro. It reminded me of the time I thrashed Jose on his front lawn. No one ever bothered me again.

I think what made me go off was thinking about the butt kicking I was going to get from my father if I came home beat up. I didn't like to fight. It just caused more trouble.

My year at Willson was not too bad. The country was being swept away with rap and break dancing, and there I was with all my fellow schoolmates rapping, beat boxing, and break dancing. And after being Zorro, I managed to have a year with very little teasing.

That same year, blessings began falling down on me. I attended a youth retreat and filled out an application to win a scholarship to Scotland. I was one of the fourteen who was chosen to go! Sure was! Out of five hundred applicants. Of those, forty were interviewed, and of those forty, fourteen were picked to go to Glasgow, Scotland, absolutely free! I was going to Scotland, and no one could believe it. In fact, I did not believe it. Might my life be getting better?

At the ninth grade award ceremony, I was acknowledged for winning the trip, and I read the essay I wrote in front of the whole school. On top of all the excitement, I was also nominated into the National Honor Society. I was the man of the hour, and it felt great. I had managed to establish a respectful reputation with the students and teachers. I will never forget Mrs. Gilliam and Mrs. Sater for all their kind words, protection, and encouragement during my stay in the "Dog House."

Willson had been the turning point in my life. I had established myself as a person and as an individual. I knew then my only ticket out of the "barrio" (ghetto) was going to be through school. Mrs. Sater kept me in line. She coached me in track, and I helped her and the volleyball team. Mrs. Gilliam was my baseball coach and my math teacher. She was hard on me, but I enjoyed it because it reminded me of the Mac where the teachers pushed me to do my best. Not only did I discover certain characteristics about myself, but I was also made aware of sex. Willson had truly been an experience.

Chapter 5
SEX

The personal aspect of my junior high year was dramatic. I had to deal with my body changes as well as my feelings about sex.

Unfortunately, I have to admit that my first exposure to sex was not very nice. The kids at Willson were very belligerent about sex. There was no decency when talking about it. I will use "we" because I admit I took part in some of the disdainful conversations. *We* talked about sex very graphically and descriptively. I always felt like a hypocrite because even though I talked a lot of stuff, I think I was the only one who had not had sex. All the bigger boys talked about it. It was the topic of every conversation it seemed. Remarks were made constantly about girls' body parts. The biggest topics concerned the buttocks and breasts. It surprised me when on one occasion the conversations involved oral sex. It was the first time I'd ever heard the term oral sex.

Understand, I considered myself a church boy. I knew what a "sin" was, and I feared God very much thanks to my mom. It bothered me to hear the boys talk so dirty because I was raised with mostly all women; my mom, Alina, and Gladys. I always thought this was indirectly a disrespect to them. Nevertheless, I participated in these conversations. Feeling like part of the group was more important to me than maintaining some anonymity.

There was a particular conversation started in the locker room. A group of boys, who were very popular in school, were getting dressed after gym class. The girls were crazy over these boys. Like Tyrone, they were the most muscular and the most athletic at Willson. With most, their reputations were based on their pecs, abs, and most importantly the size of their penis and the number of girls they had "did it with." I could not believe my ears even though I pretended to be "into" the conversation. The boys talked about doing things I could not even imagine. My eyes had been opened to sex in a way that involved phrases like "working it," and other more explicit terms. These were the words, the lingo, most used in sex conversations. It was incredible to me these boys could talk about it so openly and without shame. For me, it was culture shock.

Sex education was taught at the Mac my last year there, but it was taught to us as a very special and personal event between two people. The Mac taught us that sex was an expression of love between a man and a woman who have made a commitment to each other in the sacrament of matrimony. Inside, it bothered me to hear such dirty things, but I was also intrigued with the stories the boys told. I just could not believe some of them! It turned my thoughts of sex to such dirty and erotic mental pictures. What a transition it was to go from being a boy to being a young man. I remember exactly how the conversation began. The group of boys carried their talk all the way from gym to social studies class.

Our teacher had left the room to receive an emergency call. (I hated when teachers left the room because it became open season for the boys to gang up on quieter kids and make their lives miserable.) I felt my palms get sweaty because I knew they would start in on me. They started talking about who was and wasn't a virgin. If I could have melted away in my chair, I would have, and believe me when I say I wished I could have. I knew they would say my name out loud. I played very cool, preparing to say something sassy like, "I keep my *business* on the low so none of you know my *business*." In order to keep face with the fellas, one had to act "hard," and say sassy things in response to questions or comments being made toward or about you. There were no exceptions at Willson. It was either be "hard" or get eaten up alive.

One of the quiet boys who never bothered a soul got picked on that day. Donte was his name. He always stayed to himself and minded his own business. I will never forget what he did!

The boys started messing with him about not "getting any." Donte did not say anything at first, just trying to ignore their comments. He put his head down and pretended to read his Social Studies book. But they wouldn't quit. They kept harassing him with comments about his virginity. To get under his skin, one of the boys named Curtis commented, "Your momma was good last night." Curtis enjoyed provoking fights. He was, at the time, Willson's most popular boy.

I wanted to stand up for Donte because he was a nice boy. He never bothered anybody and always kept to himself. Since they could not break him with the comments about his mom, they began to say he had a small penis (remember, penis size was a big deal with the boys). Even the girls talked about penis sizes of their boyfriends. Some girls would go as far as to compare sizes among each other. It seemed like the girls also sat around and talked dirty. Sometimes, the conversations the girls had were raunchier than that of the boys.

When Donte could no longer take the verbal abuse, he pulled out his penis and placed it on the desk of the boy who started the whole thing...Curtis. Donte just said, "This is what Mercedes fantasizes about when she's sexing you." The room erupted! There wasn't anything anybody could say or do. We were all shocked. I had never seen a penis before, beside my own of course. And to say the least, Donte's penis was big. He just pulled it out and placed it on the desk in front of Curtis. Then, the fight erupted. Donte whipped Curtis's butt all over the Social Studies room!

I remember the way the girls responded to Donte after this incident. Donte became part of that click of cool boys. Because Donte was dark skinned, his motto at Willson became, "the darker the berry, the sweater the juice." Between the day of the fight and two weeks he totally transformed into someone else. Every time I saw him in the hallway, he had sucker bites all over his neck. Donte managed to take Mercedes, the prettiest girl at Willson, away from the boy who confronted him in the classroom about his penis...Curtis. What a shame about Donte. He was well liked by the teachers but turned into a monster. He turned into a, "cool daddy, well-endowed, you can't tell me nothing, I am the man, the mack," monster. It was amazing to me how quickly his personality changed over the incident with Curtis. It was sad to see him become part of a click I detested.

Prior to this whole ordeal, Mercedes was the proudest girl at Willson. She was going out with Curtis. He was Willson's top dog (pun intended). Curtis played basketball, football, baseball, and ran track. And according to Mercedes, he had a hell of a penis. I still believe it was hard on Mercedes keeping the other girls away from Curtis. Most of the fights involving Mercedes and other girls were about Curtis. If she only knew the things Curtis said about her behind her back. He talked openly and boldly about having sex with Mercedes. He very carefully described how he made her moan and scream when they had sex. He revealed how she'd tremble and act like she was having a seizure. I guess he was describing Mercedes having orgasms, but he was too ignorant to know what to call her "trembling and shaking.". Nonetheless, Curtis was very proud of his reputation and very proud of his penis until the day he crossed the wrong person...Donte.

My images and thoughts about sex were totally changed. At the Mac, sex was sacred and never talked about. At Willson, sex was talked about openly and without shame. It made me eager to have sex. I wanted to feel what the boys talked about. I wanted to feel what it was like, especially after it had been described as such a pleasurable experience. I wanted to make a girl shake and moan. I had become infatuated with wanting to have sex. Even though I felt these urges and I wanted to experience intimacy, something inside made me feel bad, even dirty at times. It was as though there were two people inside of me. One saying these fantasies were wrong and unchristian, while the other was dying to do it. I know now as an adult, that those fights were my spirit man battling the evil one. This was the year I discovered self-gratification, by accident.

Another occasion involving explicit bullying, the "cool boys" were making fun of one of the White kids in the locker room (it seemed all of the dirty talk happened in the locker room), after gym class (again). They taunted him about being a virgin (and it seemed like most teasing was about being a virgin). They made comments about him not ever "getting any" and having to settle by "jacking off." Guess who the ring leader was?... Donte. I asked a classmate what "jacking off' meant. He thought I was joking around. He could not believe I did not know what jacking off meant. After he described it to me, I remember thinking this must be the "pus" I had in my bed. Before attending Willson, I lived a very sheltered life. Very family orientated and church going. Willson totally changed every aspect of my innocence as a young man.

During my year at Willson, there were several occasions I was experiencing waking up at night very wet and sticky. I thought I had an infection in my penis due to the pus I saw. Well, at the time it looked like pus (I didn't know what sperm was). When this wet, sticky substance woke me up about three times a week, I had assumed it was pus due to an infection.

I was going through a period where I thought I was going to die. I knew about pus because of knee scrapes and ingrown toe nails I had in the past. During the night when I encountered what seemed to be pus by me penis, I concluded I had an infection. It happened more frequently and I began to get worried. I talked with the pastor at my church about it. He explained I was having "nocturnal emissions," better known as wet dreams. "Thank God," I thought. At one point I was convinced God was punishing me for indulging in the dreams about sex.

It became clear to me that my pus was semen and that my episodes were not an infection given to me as a punishment from God, but that it was natural and would continue to occur. I had become aware that the nights I woke up wet and sticky were the nights I dreamed about having sex or dreamed I was watching Donte and Mercedes have sex. It was fascinating to me how my dreams about Mercedes and Donte were so clear. I was amazed at how my brain could bring to life the two with such detail in my dreams.

In the dreams, I could see them wearing the same clothes they wore that day in school. Their faces and their bodies in perfect detail. In the dream, I remember hiding, watching them having sex in the locker room behind one of the shower curtains. I don't remember what they were saying. I just remember the sounds they made. I wake up. Soaked in my own sweat, tired and feeling my heart pounding in my throat.

Looking down I, felt the white sticky substance. I

remember putting Kleenex under the mattress. My biggest fear was to get caught in the middle of the night cleaning myself up. It was hard to stay quiet since our apartment wasn't that big, and it was easy to know what was going on at all times. I remember this is where I began to be as discreet as I possibly could. It had gotten to the point where I was wrapping my penis in Kleenex every night before I went to bed. The wet dreams would not be as messy as before and there was less of a chance of being caught.

After Father (the pastor) explained what was happing, to me, I could not wait for night time to come so I could conjure up my dreams. It was fabulous for me. I was actually feeling the emotions of sex without the presence of another person. I can only remember the frustrations afterwards. The only thing on my mind night and day seemed to be sex. I wanted to experience sex so badly. I wanted to be able to feel in real life what I was feeling in my dreams. I anxiously awaited my nights. It was then I least felt frustrated about being a virgin.

This part of my life was very important to me as a man. My only regret was having to experience this very crucial aspect of my sexuality in the manner in which it occurred. I often wonder if my discovery of sex would have been the same or different had I made it through St. Edward's High School.

I often wonder if another environment, another non-Black, non-inner city, non-public environment would have given me a different outlook concerning sex. Would my thoughts of sex be different? I guess I will never know the answer. I can only be grateful that I did not allow these thoughts of sex to control every aspect of my life, as I saw sex completely change the futures, especially academic futures, of some kids who attended Willson that year. If I only knew then what I know today, I would not have rushed into things. As most learning episodes happen with time, the dilemma of sex and being a virgin took care of itself all on its own as I ventured off to Glasgow, Scotland.

Chapter 6
SCOTLAND

Convincing myself I was going to Scotland was difficult. I could not believe it was actually going to happen. I hated to be so negative, but I kept thinking there must be a catch. How could God grant me this blessing despite the things and thoughts I had to offend and displease him? It was hard to accept there were no strings attached. I had actually accomplished something due to me. Winning the trip to Scotland made me realize that I was capable of doing anything as long as I put my mind to it. I remember when the teacher at the youth retreat was passing out the applications. All the kids started writing their paragraphs at the retreat in pencil. I took my application home. Father (I will refer to the pastor as Father) helped me put my thoughts onto paper much like my teachers at The Mac. He also made sure my words and sentences were grammatically correct. He allowed me to use the typewriter in the church office to type my essay. I am lucky I did not write on the application when the others did. After I finished typing up the essay, I was so proud because it looked so professional. I am assuming it was the presentation and the neatness of the application which caught the attentions of the judges. It was impressive that a 14 year old was capable of handing in such a neat application. This is what one of the judges told me after I was chosen.

This was an important step in my life. I became a strong believer in appearance and neatness. Mom always said to me that no matter where I am or wherever I go, my appearance and my neatness, and organization was a reflection of who I was. More importantly, she added, it was a reflection of the way I was raised and a reflection of my parents. "If you are disorganized, unclean, and messy, people will believe that your parents are the same. Do you want people to think your mother is a lazy, messy, unorganized, slob?" I always made sure to do things correctly, especially when I spent the night at a friend's house or when I participated in events which involved people and adults. I refused to let people think I was not being raised correctly. I had the best mom in the world and I wanted everyone to know it!

Scotland and all its wonders was an experience I will never forget. I was the baby out of the traveling bunch. The rest of the kids were in high school. I wasn't even in the 10th grade yet.

When we arrived in Glasgow, we were taken to a center where many kids came to play. Something like a city recreation center. We were the center of attention. I loved it. The kids in Scotland fascinated me. They were so different from American children. It was interesting to see the friendly interaction among the children. They played, danced, and sang songs for us. They were super friendly and very kind. The Black kids in my group were treated interestingly. The children at the center immediately thought all the Black kids could break dance, beat box and rap. They constantly asked the Black kids to do these things. One day, we sat down with them and explained to them that not all Black Americans beat box, break dance, and rap. Their stereotypes about Americans were also very fun to hear. They believed we all lived in mansions with swimming pools and expensive cars. The only popular American television programs in Scotland at the time were Dallas and Dynasty. They believed all of America was like Dallas and Dynasty and all Americans were rich and wealthy. Their accent was what we liked the most. When we first reached the center, all of us thought they were speaking a different language. It took us a while to realize they were speaking English with an accent.

Norma

I met Norma at the center. She was one of the first kids we met. I guess as word got around there were Americans in the center, more and more children came. It seemed like every day there was a new bunch of kids. Norma came about three days after we had arrived. She was beautiful. She was medium built, with blond hair, blue eyes, and very attractive. I fell in love with her from the first moment I saw her. I introduced myself to her by boldly going up to her and telling her she was very pretty. I just wanted her to accept the gesture. When she smiled and said, "Thank you." I thought I would die. Something told me I would be holding her in my arms before I left Scotland.

A week later, we took a trip to a castle in Edinboro. Norma and a group of Scottish kids went with us. I cannot remember what exactly happened that day. I just know that by evening, while we were on our way back to the center, Norma and I were holding hands resting our heads together in the cramped van. Norma was almost seventeen years old.

I was going on fifteen years old. Crazy things were happening to my insides. Every time I saw Norma, I felt sick. My stomach became queasy and my hands began to shake. She made me feel the way I felt in my dreams. It reminded me of how I felt when I dreamed about Mercedes and Donte having sex. I was too shy to do anything. But I really did not need to. Norma led, and I followed.

One evening, we had a dance at the center; Norma and I snuck off to the sleeping quarters. I remember her guiding me through the whole thing, almost as if she knew I did not know what to do. She told me to do what I felt was natural. I just wanted to kiss and hold her close to my body. I enjoyed the closeness of her breasts to my chest while I caressed her back and neck. It was embarrassing for me after a while due to my erection. Norma was fabulous at making me feel comfortable. Every time we'd kiss, I felt like I was going to bust through my skin. That evening, things became intense. We started off kissing very slowly like we'd always kiss. Kissing for me was erotic. I had never kissed anyone on the lips. It was a weird feeling. The kissing became heated, and one thing led to another as my heart raced faster and faster.

I was shocked at what was happening. I could not believe what I was doing. I was scared but at the same time excited I was finally realizing my sexual fantasy with Norma. My life was completely changed that evening. Norma and I had these sexual encounters almost every day while I was in Scotland.

The night before the departure, we snuck off to her brother's apartment. I asked Norma to have intercourse with me. I thought we were going to do it because her brother was not there. I might never see her again. I wanted to leave Scotland with the memory of having intercourse. But it wasn't just wanting to have intercourse. I was in love with Norma, and I enjoyed the closeness of her beating heart to mine.

We started off with the same kissing. I had become more bold, initiating the touching. Norma began to take off her clothes, which is something I had never seen. I'd always wondered what she looked like naked. She was beautiful to me. I was nervous about what she would think of me naked. I wasn't that muscular, but I had a decent physique.

I wanted to immediately have intercourse with Norma. I laugh now because that night I kept thinking to myself, "Is this really happening?." I was nervous about her brother walking in on us and I would never get to experience her; all of her. Norma said her brother would be out. She was very calm. Thoughts of my life instantly passed before my eyes. The excitement and love I was feeling raced through my mind. I just kept thinking that after this evening I would no longer be in the "virgin" category. And relieved that it was with someone I truly cared for.

She whispered in my ear several times she loved me, and I returned the sentiments. I did love Norma. I wanted to be with her forever. That moment and my life seemed perfect. I had finally experienced not having sex, but making love. I'd discovered and experienced sexual intercourse in an unforgettable night with a girl whom I was absolutely crazy for. I thought about the "cool boys" back at home and how they talked about their experiences so openly, so dirty like. I could never tell anybody about my night with Norma. That was a special moment between her and me. It was not at all the way I thought it would be. It was truly special. It is hard for me to conjure up those old feelings and is very difficult to write them in this memoir. Norma, to this day, is still in my heart. I still love her in my own way.

Norma and her group came to Cleveland about a week after our return. During her stay here, she spent most of her time with me. This caused a great deal of problems when it came time to taking trips with her group. It was such a problem, Norma and two of her friends were put on an airplane and sent back to Scotland prematurely. One of the directors of the program took me out to lunch to break the news to me. I went absolutely berserk in the restaurant. Dishes, plates, silverware and anything I could grab were thrown about along with loud and colorful words, tears, and pain.

Norma's friends, who stayed until the trip ended, said Norma was very upset when they forced her to the airport. They came into her room and packed her clothes by force. They took her to the airport while she was kicking and screaming my name. She implored them to let her call me to at least say goodbye, but they wouldn't let her. I was traumatized and horrified I would never see Norma again. I completely lost my mind. I stopped eating. I became very ill; I even thought about killing myself. I felt like a fish out of water. I was dead inside. I wanted to die. Nothing mattered. I was angry and felt the same rage I felt in the dream.

A few months later, I was home from school due to parents' conferences. I took in the mail; there was a letter from Norma. She asked why I had not responded to her other letters. Letters which I'd never received. Apparently, Mom was intercepting mail from Norma, and I never received them.

In her letter, she wrote she had a part of me which would never leave her. She was miserable in Scotland. She wanted to come to the U.S. She went on to say she would call on a certain day for me to be home by the phone. She never called. Finally after a year, I got a letter from one of Norma's friends who wrote to say Norma and her baby were doing great and she still planned to come to the U.S. I never heard from anyone ever again. I was left in awe, bewildered, wondering if I would ever see Norma again. I was confused and crazy to know when and by whom she had a son with. Was the baby mine? Did/do I have a son in Scotland? It is a never ending question.

It is extremely painful to recall these memories. I am reminded of the pain I felt when she left. It rekindles the bitter feelings I had toward Mom for taking my mail and never giving it to me. I believe she was protecting me from heartache and sadness by keeping Norma's letters from me. Nevertheless, Valentine's, Sweetest, and most especially Father's Day were and are the hardest times. It has been extremely painful as a teacher knowing that my "maybe" son would be the same age as my students. I realize it is so true when people say you will always love your first love. I know I always will.

Chapter 7
HIGH SCHOOL

School of the Arts

I went to Scotland two weeks after ninth grade promotion from the dog house. I had survived! I always think of what would have happened if I'd stayed at St. Edwards. I would never have gotten to see Scotland or fall in love. The friends I had from Mac were out of my life. Most of them knew I withdrew from St. Edwards, and ever since, I had little or no contact with any of them. It was hard dealing with the fact that most of the friends from the Mac were making it in private school. People would tell me with a private school background I could get into any college of my choice.

It was said that public school kids were lucky just to graduate out of high school and get a job somewhere. It ate at me night and day as I questioned my decision to leave St. Edward. Should I have given up? Did I give up too quickly?

Should I have put up a fight? I wanted to go to college and was terribly scared I would not receive a solid education from the public schools or be prepared for college with a public education. During the end of the year at Willson, the school board sent applications home for those children who wanted to take part in the new magnet schools the system was trying out. I selected the School of the Arts. I had always wanted to be in a school like "Fame." I contacted the school and set up an audition.

When I auditioned for the School of Arts, I was terrified. I must have watched every episode of Fame to prepare myself for the audition. I really wanted to attend CSA (Cleveland School of the Arts). I practiced a scene from the "West Side Story" over and over. I wanted to knock their socks off. Since the audition required a song, I decided to be different. I sang "This Day" by Jennifer Holiday and signed the words. My next door neighbor was deaf; he helped me with the sign language.

I felt good about my audition. There were about ten kids the day I auditioned. The school was old, dusty, and worn down but it had a sense of warmth. I noticed the artwork and photos on the wall my first day there. The art pieces gave me a sense of compassion and a fierce sense of talent.

The students obviously loved their school and their work. Although the walls and ceilings were falling down, it made no difference. This was an old school with spirit and love on the walls and hallways. It could be felt from every corner, every staircase, and every classroom.

By walking in the building, one could actually feel the energy. It's hard to describe, but you could feel the excitement at CSA; this is where my heart told me I had to come.

The older kids from the school were present at the auditions. They were so nice. They made me feel so comfortable. I remember one of the students telling me the key to getting in CSA was to impress the theater teacher, Mr. Fisher (he auditioned the students). He told me Mr. Fisher looked for focus, volume, and confidence in the students. I felt like I was cheating because this student was not giving anybody else any hints or suggestions. Although it was my first audition ever, I learned so much. It was an experience, an exciting experience like the interview I had for the trip to Scotland.

I remember the tension I felt in the audition room. The anxiety I felt made me perform better. I have always worked best under pressure or in tense moments. I learned to use my anxiety and my nervousness to my advantage. It took control and confidence and believing I could do it. After the audition, I felt so relieved. Thank God that boy was there the day I auditioned. It would not have turned out as well, I think. I never saw the student again. I even looked for him the following September. No one looked like the young man that gave me the advice at the audition. He probably was my guardian angel.

When I returned from my trip to Scotland, I had forgotten all about my audition. I was reminded when I received a notice in early August from the Board of Education. I read the first few words before I began yelling and screaming with joy. All I can remember was, "Dear William, I am pleased to inform you that you have been selected to the Magnet School for the Performing Arts. ..." There was no question I was having the best year of my life. Nothing went wrong. I had survived the worst middle school in the system, I went to Scotland, I fell in love, made love and to top off the summer, I was accepted into the most popular new school in the system.

I was delighted to go to a high school where there would be no kids from Willson. I had a chance to start fresh. New friends, and a new perspective on life. I wanted to put my experiences from my trip abroad to use. I felt as if I had matured and was eager to have new relationships, new friendships.

The spirit at CSA was incredible. I quickly made new friends. These were not at all like the kids at Willson. Even today, I am convinced CSA was a school where it was okay to be and act as one wanted. It was difficult for me to change my "hard," bad boy attitude. It became so embedded at Willson. It was second nature. At Willson, in order to survive, I had to put up a front or be beaten up and harassed constantly.

CSA was a place to be open, alive, and unafraid to show emotions. Acting, singing, art, dancing, and playing an instrument was the way to let go of inhibitions and timidness. I was fascinated with the sounds in the building. It was impressive, especially what went on in the hallways; students rehearsing songs, tuning instruments, warming up for dance class, and students running lines from plays. It was a true feeling of work and pride. I jumped right in! I declared theater for my major. Mr. Fisher was my theater teacher. He taught me everything about theater. I fell in love with CSA. I fell in love with acting and directing. I was proud to be part of the student body and proud to be part of such a wonderful class. My very own "Fame" had come to fruition.

Sophomore

Sophomore year was incredible. I landed a supporting role in the musical of the year called "Dracula Baby." I played the part of Renfield. I discovered acting along with all the aspects of the stage and performing. I came alive in my major. Slowly, I began to drop my guards from Willson and allowed myself to be built and molded by Mr. Fisher. It wasn't all just fun and games though. Mr. Fisher was my mentor, my inspiration, my teacher, and friend. He convinced me of my talents and helped me to perfect my craft.

Outside of school, I began performing in community theaters. I auditioned for my first show outside of CSA at the Community College. I was given the role of Young Saige in "Bubbling Brown Sugar." Mr. Fisher and some other teachers from elementary and middle school like Mrs. Jones from Case, Mrs. Kennard from the Mac, and Mrs. Sater from Willson, came to see me perform.

Mrs. Kennard was especially proud of me. I was her actor in the seventh and eighth grade at the Mac. I played the lead in "No Vacancy" my seventh grade year and Joseph my eighth grade year in "Joseph and His Amazing Technicolor Dream Coat." Now that I think about it, my acting career began due to Mrs. Kennard's confidence in me and her casting me as the lead both those years. Mrs. Kennard was a teacher I will never forget from Mac.

Her favorite saying was, "School is not for me, it's for you." I never knew what that meant until I went to college. And you know something? She was right! School was the key to getting out of the ghetto. Even though sometimes I hated going, even though sometimes I didn't get along with some of my teachers, it was school which got me where I am today.

At CSA, I learned to make school work for me. I took CSA for whatever I could. I learned an appreciation for the Arts and all the hard work that goes into a production or talent. My eyes were opened to life as it was. I learned to interpret different roles, making them come to life. I studied people, and human behavior by observing strangers in public places such as malls and bus stations. Learning to view life as a role, life as a play, and all people as the actors in that play was a wonderful realization. The stage and the lights became home. I was comfortable and at peace there. I was whole there. CSA steered my life and pointed me in the right directions. My experiences both under the lights and in real life made situations more comprehensible and easier to deal with, especially in difficult times and situations. Theater brought a whole new meaning to situations, pressures, stress, family problems, and problems concerning myself and who I was.

I became known as "Spanky" to those at CSA. A good person to my friends. A loyal and dedicated confidant to those who grew near to my heart. Loved and cared for by my peers. Looked at as a person with enthusiasm and one that had the will to make it in life. What a role God had given me. And it kept building. In January of 1986, I was nominated President of my class. I learned then that God was not a mean God. He did not sit around in clouds waiting to punish me. He was a good God, a faithful God, and a God that would never let me down.

Junior

Every year at CSA, I felt as if though I had reached a higher level in my world both good and bad. Although my home life was in a complete upheaval, my Junior year was phenomenal! Again, I was voted as president of my class and representative of the school for the Leadership Cleveland program of Northern Ohio called "Look Up To Cleveland," and founder of CSA's only team, the volleyball squad. In our very first year of competition, CSA won its division and placed second in the championship. In theater, my classmates and I auditioned to win a theater scholarship for acting at The Chautauqua Institute in New York. It was Mr. Fisher who informed me two weeks after the audition I was the sole full scholarship recipient in the entire State of Ohio. I would spend the summer learning more about acting in one of the world's most prestigious institutions. I felt so blessed! I was overwhelmed after receiving the good news. All of my classmates were so happy for me. It was wonderful feeling support from my friends. How refreshing it was to see my friends sharing in my excitement.

Chautauqua

Chautauqua was a life-long experience. Meeting William Hurt and Sabrina Le Beauf (the oldest sister on the Cosby Show) was a lifelong experience The theater company of three groups consisted of high school students called "Studio II ," the college theater students called the "Conservatory," and the group of professional actors. The "professionals" were running a show called, "The Lion In Winter." Later in college at a movie theater, I saw Tony Goldwyn, one of the actors from this group. He played the bad guy in the movie "Ghost" with Demi Moore and Patrick Swazie. It was Mother's Day when I first saw "Ghost." I leaped out of my chair in the dark and crowded theater and yelled, "Mom,

Mom, Oh my God, I know him." Needless to say, I was highly embarrassed, and of course no one believed me.

Fatima, a girl I was best friends with in Studio II, was the second exciting surprise that year. She was the only Black girl in our group I hung around with. Fatima and I did a scene on our grand scene night from, "A Raisin In The Sun." We received a thunderous applause unlike any other applause I was ever given. I discovered Fatima on "New York Undercover" playing the ex-wife of the Black police officer played by Malik Yoba. I still had her number from that summer, so I called to tell her how excited I was to see her on the show. I left her a voicemail but Fatima never returned my call.

A thousand scenarios ran through my head: Did she think I was trying to get a hook up? Had she torn her ties with all the little people who hadn't gotten their big break? Maybe she was just too busy. I wondered if I'll ever see Fatima on the big screen. And when I did, would people believe she and I were the stars of Studio II that summer in Chautauqua? We were a hit, and to two high school kids, it was a big deal to be the only students chosen to perform in two scenes. Fatima and I were congratulated by the entire company with small cards and notes on the night of the Studio II show; we were so blessed at Chautauqua. To be the minority of the high school group and to have the honor of performing twice that evening was great. The possibilities of acting were turning wheels in my head. But was the courage to make an attempt in my heart? It was an exciting feeling as well as a terrifying one. Maybe my last year at CSA would help me find the road to where I wanted to go.

Senior

Senior year was awful all the way around. Home life went from bad to worse and the thought of leaving CSA mad me sick to my stomach. I was scared about graduation and saying goodbye to my family at school. I practically lived at the school. I sang in the Gospel Choir after school, or would stay around and help out with costumes or productions. CSA was my security blanket. It was the place where my dreams came true. I did not want my days at CSA to end. My classmates were my brothers and sisters. I became terrified of losing them and the relationships we had built in three years.

In the spring of my senior year, it became evident that graduation was close at hand. Everyone was busy working a job for prom and graduation or working to help out with tuition for the following year in college. Since I had learned my lesson with the St. Edward ordeal, I figured why lie to myself? My parents could not afford college. And Lord knows where I got the cockied idea to apply to the United States Naval Academy. Appointed by

Louis Stokes, I was all ready to sign. But Mom was not having it. She refused to see me become part of the government. She told me I had to go to college if she had to work night and day. She refused to see me in a military uniform. Knowing it would make her happy, I began applying to colleges. Ohio State, Morehouse and Ashland were my first choices. Ohio State didn't offer me any scholarships or grants for theater while Morehouse was out of the question for Mom because of the distance from home, so when Ashland accepted me, and offered me a Theater Scholarship I said yes. It was close to home yet far enough that I could lose myself if I needed.

Saying goodbye to CSA was saying goodbye to my friends and my life. CSA was my life. Acting, directing and dancing were my life. I had to prepare myself for a new change. A whole new start again. None of my classmates applied to Ashland. I'd start fresh and all alone. I had to prepare for yet another change in my life. I would be going from an all-Black, inner city surrounding, to a rich, private, uppity and all white college environment.

My teachers and friends would tell me I had a bright future in store for myself. That gave me confidence. I was steadfast in my goals, and the steps to achieving them were clear to me. I knew it would be a battle, but I felt with the training I had received at CSA, church, and the different groups I belonged to, I was ready for difficult times if the presented themselves to me. I did not know how I would pay for school. I was afraid after graduation my parents would not be able to afford college. Who was I kidding? In fact, I knew they could not afford it. That was very clear to me. My father was working at a factory and Mom continued to work at the May Company making enough to pay the rent and have food on the table. It wasn't until later those things became awful. The tragedies that followed completely ruined what had been the best three years of my life.

Chapter 8
ALL AT ONCE

I became very close to the Father at my church. He was like a dad to me. He helped me make decisions about college and my future. Father also helped me out financially. He gave me small jobs in the church, waxing the floors, setting up for after-service coffee and doughnuts, shoveling snow, painting, and other odds and ends.

The summer following junior year, I was painting the church hall when I received a telephone call from the police department. It struck me odd because no one really knew where I was that day. When the officer explained what had happened, I went numb. I felt as if someone had poured a bag of ice in my stomach. My insides felt cold and tight. It was my father. He had been in an automobile accident and was asking for his family. The officer said it was very serious and suggested I should get to the hospital as soon as possible. Of course, I was painted from head to toe and didn't have keys to lock the church, and Father was nowhere to be found. I just left. I thought to myself, "I have to get outta here." The whole way to the hospital, I kept thinking his accident was my fault. For years I kept wanting, wishing for something bad to happen to him. I wanted him to suffer a little for all the times he had made me suffer.

From what I understood, my father was somehow shoved off the side of the road by a truck. Apparently, the car twisted off the highway and flipped over a couple times. The doctors explained to Mom that he had to be wedged out of the car since he was pinned underneath. There was no sense in asking if he was wearing a seatbelt because we knew he wasn't. My father never wore a seatbelt. Or, let's just say I never saw him put one on.

The car landed upside down. Since he was not wearing a seat belt, he was tossed around the car. He had internal bleeding caused by a ruptured spleen, all of his ribs on the right side of his body were either broken or fractured, and his heart and lungs were badly bruised from the steering wheel and being flung around like a rag doll. The surgeon instructed Mom to go in and see him and to send us in one by one. They were going to operate to stop the bleeding. The concern was his heart and lungs being too weak to undergo an operation.

He looked like a monster! There were tubes sticking out of him everywhere! He was all cut up from the front windshield of the car. His face was covered with lines, and there were huge bumps by his eyes and on his forehead. It was an absolutely horrifying thing to see him lying there between life and death. It looked as though someone had dipped him in a pool of blood. He was completely drenched. It was a miracle he pulled through. The way he looked on his way to the operating room has been embedded in my mind and will always be picture clear. He was not supposed to survive but he did. I believe divine intervention and Alina's faith in the Holy mother, The Virgin Mary, helped to save him.

A miracle?

After Alina made her first communion, she was given a bible and a statue of Mother Mary from Father. She gave the statue to my father for his car. Alina told him Mary would protect him. My father put the tiny brown statue on the dash of the car. I remember on several occasions when it was just him and me in the car, he complained about the statue not staying on the dash. He constantly picked it up off the floor from between the gas and the brake pedals. Every time he turned the corner, the statue would fall to the floor of the car. He told Alina he was going to take the statue inside and put it on the dresser in his room. Alina did not object, but by the look on her face you could tell she was sad that my father did not want to keep it in the car. My father never brought the statue in the house from the car. I think he dealt with the frustration of the statue to spare Alina's sad face.

When we finally located the junk yard where the car had been towed, we were shocked! The car was completely squashed. How could anyone have survived that accident? It looked as though the car had been demolished by a compression machine. We were convinced Mother Mary saved my father when we saw her statue on the dash of the car. Just standing there like nothing ever happened! There was no way that little statue could have remained on the dash after all the tumbling and turning the car had been through. It's hard to believe someone took the time out to place the statue on the exact location where my father had her. It was a miracle! It had to have been a miracle!

After the surgery, the doctors said he would make it but needed to remain on the respirator and heart monitor for safety precautions. They wanted to monitor his lungs to make sure they would not collapse. I remember the lung exercise machine with the little ball in it. My father had to blow into the small tube. The object was to make the little white ball go as high as it could. At the beginning, he couldn't get the little ball past the first line. After about a week, the little white ball began to go higher and higher. This meant his lungs were getting stronger. It took a while before he could talk since the tubes from the operation caused some stress in his throat.

According to his doctors, my father would need help with many things. We were to prepare ourselves for helping him to walk, dress, and bathe him. The hospital gave him a walker to assist him in getting around. During his hospital stay, our friends from church came over to the house to pray the Rosary. It was enjoyable to have company in our house since we were rarely visited by anyone. For nine days, people came over to pray with us. Mom explained in Spanish countries it is customary of Latinos to pray the Rosary. It is a Latino custom and tradition, especially during hard times, for the community to pull together and pray "El Rosario." Even strangers came over (friends of friends from my church) with food, cards, and money to show their support and offer their prayers to my family. It was special for me to experience my community's response to the horrible accident my father experienced. It made me feel as if though the church was part of my family. It was a good feeling to know we were not alone during such difficult moments. I was relieved God had not let him die. I would not have been able to live knowing his accident was my doing.

As the days went by, things got worse and worse. My father was unable to return to work. Prior to the car accident, my father was working on his workman's compensation for an accident he had at the factory. He injured his back trying to hold up some merchandise which almost fell off a tow motor onto a worker sitting at a machine. I remember the accident clearly because we had to pick him up from the emergency room the day it happened. The person he saved could not hear him yelling to move out of the way. My father ran over and held the merchandise with his arms while another person got the attention of the worker sitting underneath. Luckily, my father could hold on long enough to allow the worker to leave his seat. I understand it was seconds that saved the man's life. Although he injured his back, he was hailed a hero. After the accident, he continued to work in a lighter capacity. It wasn't until a friend told my father he could file for workman's compensation that he did.

Welfare

There was no money, and once again Mom had to take on the role of provider. She worked two jobs. In addition to the May Company job, she cleaned offices at a downtown office building. Things had gotten so bad that our electricity was cut off. A month later, the gas was also cut off.

We went a couple of days surviving on "arepas" (corn flower bread) and cheese. My father finally decided to go to welfare after debating it with Mom.

It was humiliating for my parents! It was embarrassing for us kids. Welfare was something the kids at school talked about all the time. Usually, the kids that were the poorest and did not dress the best were said to be on "welfare." It was terrible to be on welfare, especially when it seemed like everyone at church and in the neighborhood knew about it. I remember dreading to go grocery shopping. It was so embarrassing paying for the food with food stamps. Our neighborhood supermarket was so small it seemed everyone stared at us when it was time to go to the cashier. I remember doing everything possible to avoid going to the cashier. Sometimes, I would make myself sick so that I would get sent to the car and wait until the groceries were paid for. The worst part was getting a cashier who yelled aloud, "That'll be forty dollars in stamps, ten dollars in merchandise."

By now, things had gotten so bad that the arguments were daily, and over the smallest things. Mom was angry at the world, and my father hit rock bottom. He started to drink more and more. The worst part was Mom and my father had just taken out a loan for the house we lived in. The biggest arguments were about the money for the mortgage payments.

Those were the worst of all because everyone felt guilty. It was unheard of to ask for toys or anything that wasn't a pure necessity. There was just no way we could afford any extra things. Times had really gotten rough. We had never been as poor as we were after the accident. Christmas, birthdays, Easter outfits and trips to the mall and the amusement parks were totally out. Thank God I was so involved at church.

Father

Every summer, the church planned excursions to different places. Because I was an altar boy, I and the other alter boys went free of charge. Father took us to Cedar Point, an amusement park, Canada and the water slide park. I have realized that my church and Father were responsible for a great majority of my childhood being complete. By complete I mean going to places and having experiences any child should have in their childhood. For two summers, Father asked my mom if it would be alright for me to go away to camp for a week. At camp, I forgot about all the problems. I learned to ride a horse, shoot a bow and arrow, swim and cheer. It was a fabulous time. I hated when it was the end of the week at camp because it meant coming back to the real world.

To reality. To all the problems. I think Father was concerned about the summer and being at home with all the arguments and fighting. Father always found something for me to do. I guess he knew if my mind was occupied it would help me forget some of the problems happening at home.

I was either at camp or at the church painting, cleaning, or learning how to fix something. Father taught me a great many things.

Father was in the Navy and came from a very rural background.

It seemed to me that he knew a little of everything. He knew how to fix things when they were broken and explained why things should be done a certain way. I appreciate the things I learned from Father. The part I most appreciated was he always made the question "Why" clear in every situation. Whether it was raking the leaves so the gutters would not get clogged, or cleaning the candle holders so the wax would not harden and become difficult to clean, or maybe something simple like why the floors of the church hall needed to be mopped down before applying the cleaning chemicals and wax.

With Mom, and especially my father, chores always came across as slave work. It seemed at times like work assigned by my father was simply invented for the sake of seeing me work. But now, I understand this was just my father's way of showing me how to be a man. But again, I wonder why my father simply didn't explain "why?" I did chores because I was told to do them. No questions asked!

I remember the first time I saw Father angry was during winter. Before mass, I came over to shovel the snow as I normally did when it snowed. It was routine for me to get the keys from him for the church where the shovels and salt were kept. I wasn't thinking about the keys; I just begun shoveling the snow like I had always done before. After mass, when he asked me for them, I reached into my pocket. They were not there! Gone! They were gone! Father was furious. He must have shoveled snow for two hours. He'd take a shovel full of snow and throw it up against the tree trunk in front of the rectory hoping the keys would hit the tree and make a noise. The ring contained keys to the house, church, rectory and every lock in all the buildings. After about three hours we went in the rectory for some hot chocolate. Father calmly explained the importance of paying attention to detail and being aware of where important things are at all times. Father did warn me several times to keep track of the keys. Believe me when I say from then on, I began to focus on important things like keys, watches, rings, eye glasses and other things. To this day, when I misplace something simple like my class rings, my house and car keys, or even something as daily as the remote to the cable and T.V., I remember the day I lost the keys to the church. It reminds me how horrible and helpless I felt the day I lost the church keys. I find myself designating places for things or returning objects to their proper place. Lessons like these I credit to Father. These are lessons young people should learn, but in a manner in which it doesn't make the person feel guiltier, dehumanized or humiliated. This is the way I find myself teaching my students.

The Lawsuit

The woes continued. As if the accident, welfare, and all the fighting wasn't enough, there was the lawsuit.

Although the majority of the arguments were about finances, or better yet the lack of money, there was the lawsuit against Mom and my father from the previous owner of our home. From what I gathered, my father made a side deal with the previous owner for a couple thousand dollars. The point of the deal was to compensate the previous owner for the difference in his desired selling price. The previous owner wanted $17,000.00 for the house my father and Mom bought from him. But the bank only appraised the house for $1 5,000.00. My father signed an I.O.U. with the previous owner for the $2,000.00 difference. Before the accident, my father was paying him monthly installments. After his car accident, there was no way my father could continue the monthly payments. The previous owner took my parents to court.

The ordeal ended vaguely. The whole thing was kept from us, Gladys, Alina, and me. I guess Mom did not want to add to our problems. Mom wasn't stupid; she could tell the problems and the dysfunction in the family was affecting us not only in the house but also at school.

Because of the lawsuit, Mom went through garnishment of her wages and the humiliation of being in a courtroom during the whole ugly ordeal. She was indignant with my father for the lawsuit. She could not believe he made a side deal with the previous owner and kept it a secret from her. I can only imagine how betrayed she felt. She was angry at my father for all he put us through with the lawsuit. It was frightening for me, especially when the previous owner came to visit our next door neighbors. He'd lean up against our front gate and talk aloud about how one day he would get his money *and* his house back. One day, my father was in the house listening to all the comments he was making. When he couldn't take it anymore, he charged out of the front door. This happened several times until one day, my father and the previous owner were inches from a fight in the street. Had it not been for the police and the neighbors, it would have been ugly. A fight never happened, but Mom swears to this day, and is convinced, the previous owner had something to do with my father's automobile accident.

Mom's wages continued to be garnished until they closed down the May Company. Mom lost her job and became more irate with my father, especially now that she was the only one working. Our only means of survival was welfare. Mom and my father hardly spoke two words to each other in the house. It was so frightening because anything could set them off; the toilet seat being left up, a light switch left on or something as simple as taking your shoes off when entering the house.

Mom was a fanatic with cleanliness. It drove her mad to see the house in disarray. Since she worked, Gladys kept up with the house and made sure it was clean before Mom got home from work. Sometimes, Gladys and Mom would fight because Mom would redo everything Gladys had tried to clean; like the floors or the dishes. Mom complained about working and having to come home to clean up in addition to working a whole day's work. There was no washer and no money to go down to the laundry mat, so Mom washed all of our clothes in the tub. She would remind us of her raw fingers and how we did not appreciate her hard work. She'd constantly say we treated her like a maid. Her favorite line was she was going to disappear and never come back. She'd say one day she would fall asleep and never wake up. She'd tell us it would be our fault when it happened. It was frightening to hear her talk like that. All I could think about was how horrible it would be if my father was the only parent in the house. I would lay awake at night making sure Mom was breathing. I'd stare at her covers for hours and hours making sure that I saw them move. I remember feeling relieved to see her covers move from her respiration. I'd pray over her as she slept the night away.

All of this stress was becoming evident at school. I was constantly scolded for sleeping during lessons. There were more problems with teachers and myself. I turned into a monster. I began to slack in my school work and would find any opportunity to get into fights and arguments with my teachers and my friends. My close friends constantly asked what was wrong, but I shut them out. There was no way I could tell my family problems. It wasn't something I did. Mom and my father always told us the problems of the home stay in the home and never go outside the home. That rule was sacred and was never meant to be broken, until the day I exploded.

One of my teachers refused to let me in a class because the bell had rung. I became so enraged and angry I punched and kicked the lockers outside the room. My History teacher, Mr. Steinmetz, darted out of his classroom to grab me and calm me down. I could tell by the expression on his face I had frightened him. His eyes were big, and he had such a worried expression on his face. I was so furious! Not letting me in the room had done it. I went OFF! I was yelling every bad word I could think of. I felt as though I had to get a demon out of me. My eyes were full of tears and saliva was around my mouth and on my chin. I would not talk. I couldn't! I was so enraged. It was the feeling in the dream all over again.

It was a paralyzing feeling. My brain wanted to talk but nothing would come out. There were no words. I remember feeling a great sense of relief even though I was in a tirade. The feeling was like holding your breath under water and quickly coming to the surface for air. It was a good feeling to finally release all the tension, anxiety, stress, and anger I managed to build up. People asked me questions, but I refused to say anything. I was so overwhelmed with anxiety and frustration that my desire for words was numb. Later in the lounge, my closest friends came to be with me. They did not ask me what was wrong. They simply walked in and hugged me. They came to tell me they were there for me. For the first time in my life, I felt as though my friends were true. I was convinced they were sincere and meant what they'd said. The last time I felt I really had a friend was Tyrone, and that was almost seven years ago. I finally let it all out. I told everything. I completely spilled my guts. After about two hours of blabbering away, everyone in the lounge was crying. They could not believe what I was telling them. I told them everything. I told them everything from my father's abuse toward me, to dealing with the uncertainty about having a son, to dealing with all the fighting at home due to money and the lawsuit. They could not believe I was able to function with all the problems I was keeping inside. My closest girl friend, Michelle, told me I was a strong person to be able to endure so much pain and still be able to come to school and act as if everything was fine. People used to tell me they envied me for my life, carefree spirit, enthusiasm and my popularity. I don't think anyone knew the pain I was carrying. I was dealing with a lot, but I was putting my best acting skills to use. If people would have known who the real me was, they sure as hell would not have wanted to be like me...at all!

The pressures became too demanding. Being president of the class, captain of the team, trying to work a job to support my personal needs, the expenses for prom and college, and dealing with the nightmare of being attacked was too much for me to handle. The pressure did me in. I couldn't take it anymore. I had exploded!

From that day forward, my friendship with the people who came to see me remained solid, faithful, sacred, and meaningful. I will never forget the Michelle(s), Danita, Tammy, David, Omari, and Mr. Steinmetz. Where was I ever going to have friends like the friends I had at CSA? They were my second family. It became more difficult to accept graduation.

As I became moody, I lost many friends. The worst part was all the bridges I burned with my teachers. My grades dropped significantly, and my basic attitude was "Screw it." I thank God almighty for Michelle. She told me if she had not known me as well as she did, our friendship would have ended a long time ago. She was understanding. I could talk to her about anything, like with Tyrone. I even shared with her my deepest and scariest secret. A secret which she later learned. Later, as in three years later. I could not bring myself to tell anyone about the night I was attacked.

For several months, I toiled with the decision to write about the other major trauma I sustained. A traumatic experience which caused a drastic personality change in me and great unhappiness. I was horrified to release this secret since I had kept it to myself for so many years. It was a decision I've teetered with for a very long time.

Chapter 9
WHY ME?

During my explosion in the lounge, I unwittingly blurted out something which made someone ask me to repeat what I had said. It was one of those situations when something you want no one to know simply "slips out." There was no way I could ever tell anyone what happened to me the night of the Indian's home opener. I did my best to play it off, never really going into detail about the night I was attacked. Thank God those in the lounge didn't pry for an elaborate explanation. I managed to get out of explaining what happened to me. The attack was still too fresh in my mind, and the last thing I wanted to do was relive that horrible night. It was extremely too painful and personal at the time.

What happened to me the night of the baseball home opener was the single most major crisis I was trying to handle, trying to forget, trying to accept and most importantly trying to hide. I was attacked by a couple of men on my way home from the stadium.

Omari and I worked the rally before the game. My mentor from "Look up to Cleveland" invited me and a friend to the Indians yearly rally before the start of the home opener. I took Omari. We were asked to serve free hot dogs and pop to the public. It was such a wonderful event. Some of the Indians came by to say hello to the crowd which gathered right outside the stadium before the game. There were balloons, bumper stickers, post cards, and other little things for the public which were all free. It was a fun time. Omari and I had a blast. After the rally, we were given free tickets to the game.

During the game, Omari looked awfully sick. He kept leaving to go to the bathroom. After the seventh inning stretch, he asked if we could go. I was excited about the game since it was my first major league game and the Indians were winning. The stands were packed and the crowd was having a blast. I told Omari to go on without me since he was not feeling well. I remember he was eating the free hot dogs like crazy. He probably had a little too much during the rally. I did not mind him leaving. I told him to go on home and I would call him later on to check if he was feeling better. It was no big deal! I just wanted to stay the whole game and watch the Indians win.

The Indians won the game in the ninth inning. One of the players hit a home run. The crowd went berserk! The game ended in the early evening. Leaving the stadium with the thousands of fans was exciting. I had become an Indians fan. I even bought an

Indians cap, a T-shirt and a giant balloon for my sister. I remember thinking it would be a nice gesture on my part.

I realized when I reached the bus stop, I had only some change left. There was hardly enough for bus fare, so I decided to walk home. It was a beautiful evening. The weather was warm, and I was so elated about the game. It never occurred to me that I should stop and call home or have someone pick me up. I thought my father would fuss about the "after game traffic," and Mom did not have her car, so I just footed it. It was no biggie since I had walked from downtown many times before. It wasn't far from where I lived, and besides, it wasn't the first time.

About halfway home, I felt I was being followed. I knew I wasn't crazy because the same van kept circling the avenue where I was walking. The first time someone whistled and yelled out, "Yo, baby," I kept on walking, but I crossed the street. I remember thinking there were hardly any automobiles that night. I thought to myself, "What am I going to do if this van turns around again? Should I run? Should I continue walking and hope they drive off? Should I ignore them and pray they leave me alone?" I was numb with fear. I do remember bringing the old me out. The old me from junior high school. The hard look, the tough walk and my "Don't screw with me" body language.

From that point on, it's a blur of bits and pieces. Maybe it's because all these years I have tried to forget about it. Now, I understand how people can block things out of their minds. It is just wanting to believe it never happened. It's wanting to make sense of a horrid dream which inevitably turns out to be death deifying, unimaginable and real life. One does their best to convince themselves it wasn't as bad as it looks or feels, but deep down within your soul of souls, you just cannot explain how it happened or why it happened or that it happened and happened to you. This is the type of thing you see in a movie or hear about in big cities like New York or L.A. To this day, I still have trouble believing it happened to me.

My life passed before my eyes when the van pulled up beside me facing the opposite direction of traffic. All I could think about was hoping a police car would see the van on the wrong side of the road and come over to see what this van was doing facing the wrong way. The ironic part was I was only a couple of blocks from the police station.

I close my eyes and still smell the inside of the van. It was the same smell from the club house I had in my garage. I remember the old carpet the kids and I laid on the floor of the garage. It became wet and moldy. After a week, an odor came from the carpet. The same odor was in the van. The smell of wet carpet.

I prayed inside my head for God to take care of me. I thought about my mom and my sisters. I thought about the School of Arts. I wondered in an instant who would come to my funeral. Who would find me? Would I be found? Why was this happening to me? In my head, I prayed the Our Father and the Hail Mary in Spanish over and over again. I wanted the ordeal to be over fast and painless. I wanted to go straight to heaven. I asked myself if I deserved heaven. Would I go to heaven? Had I been good enough to be allowed in heaven? Or would I have to go to purgatory for all the bad thoughts and intentions I had concerning my father and the people in my life that I disliked or could not get along with. For an instant, I was amazed at all the things going on in my head. I even remember thinking this is what people mean when they say, "I saw my whole life pass before my eyes."

I felt bad for having the dream about killing my father. I felt guilty about the sexual dreams I kept having and wanting to have sex. I felt I might not go to heaven for allowing myself to like the exotic dreams and wanting to have them every night. God would ask me about all these things. What would I say? How would I plead my case and be allowed into heaven?

I was punched several times in the mouth and kicked in the buttocks. One of the men forced me to the floor of the van and yelled for me to lie on my stomach without moving. I recall more than one person in the van because I felt the van moving while there was a knee in the small of my back. There had to have been more than one male. All the while, I smelled beer on one of their breaths. They were drunk. I could also remember bottles banging into each other as the van slowed down and picked up speed. I consoled my fear by saying to myself, "They just want to scare me and will let me go."

The van pulled into some rocky ground. I could feel the tires hitting and going over the holes and the rocks. When the van stopped, I thought this was it. They would beat me up some more and throw me out of the van.

I felt arms going around my waist as I lay terrified on my stomach. At first, I thought I was being picked up or something. But something strange was happening. I was lifted off the floor so that I was on all fours like a crawling baby. The hands returned to my waist but were now touching my genitals. The hands aggressively moved on my genitals. The person began saying nasty things to me. I could not believe what was happening. My first intentions were to urinate on purpose. I thought they were sure to leave me alone if I urinated on myself. But I figured it would make them mad and I'd probably get beaten up more than what I had already gone through. The hands began tugging at my belt. Once it was unfastened, I felt my zipper go down and my pants unbuckle. I wanted to die. I just kept praying inside my head over and over.

The pain I endured for the next period of time was unbearable. My buttocks were numb from all of the hitting and the slapping. The pain reminded me of the time I was swatted at Willson by one of the teachers for talking back and being disrespectful during a lesson. My knees were scraped up from the carpet and the pressure I put on them when I was being raped by the two men. My nipples hurt me so bad; the simple rubbing of the shirt against them was painful. They were pulled and bitten and sucked by one of the men while the other sodomized me. The two then switched positions after a while went past, and it went on for what seemed to be an eternity. It burned as if my anus had been set on fire. I had never felt such enormous pain. I just wanted to die. I asked God to make me stop breathing; I just wanted to die to stop the pain.

The last dose of punches and kicks came just before I felt the cool air. I could hear the doors of the van opening. This was it. I was either going to be killed or thrown out of the van and then be killed. I was still in the van when it began to move. All of a sudden, I felt more darkness. It was an awkward feeling since I had been blindfolded the entire time! It was totally black and interestingly, I felt no pain. I think I was knocked unconscious.

When I woke up, I still had the blindfold over my eyes. I discovered later it was gray tape and two maxi pads. I was terrified to take the blindfold off. I was afraid the men would be right there when I took off the blindfold. I removed the tape slowly. It hurt to peel the tape away from my hair, but that was the least of my hurt. My ribs, lower back and face felt like a throbbing heart. The worst pain was on my buttocks and anal cavity. It was unimaginable that I had lived. It was unbelievable to me to still have my life. Even though I was horrified about the whole ordeal, I began to cry and thank God that I would see my friends and my family again.

Arriving home is still fuzzy. I honestly can't remember how I got there. I only remember thinking how was I going to explain the way I looked to my family.

I attributed the whole overwhelming ordeal to a fight. I told my mom I had been jumped on the way home from the game. Period. For nine years, this is what everyone believed happened that horrible night.

I've always wondered how my father would react. I know Mom would just ask why I didn't tell her what happened. I just didn't want to go through police, investigations, and giving this an opportunity to reach the school, neighbors or even the newspaper. I was going through enough. I simply didn't want to go through more than what those two sons of bitches put me through. The family was going through enough; this would have killed my mom.

I've dealt with all the emotions all these years. I have asked myself "why?" a trillion times. Why me? What was it about me that attracted the van? Was it the way I was walking? Was it some type of body language or gesture? I kept thinking it must have been the same things that made the kids at school and in the neighborhood call me gay and a fag. But what? I have been told it's the mannerism in my walk, the gestures my hands make, and how I sound when I talk. But I couldn't help it. It's who I was, who I've always been. Maybe these characteristics stem from all the women in my life. My mom, my sisters, and the majority of my teachers and friends were all women. Could that have been it? Was being surrounded by women all my life affecting my manly traits?

I went from being confused to feeling pity and feeling very angry at myself. Growing up, I forced myself to accept that what happened that evening was not my fault. I guess writing about what happened to me that horrible night helps to finally cope with it. It was time to finally let it all out, even if only on paper. I can't believe I have allowed myself to relive that nightmare. It's good though, I think, because it is no longer bottled up inside of me.

The situations with my father, my sisters, and the bullies in my life were horrible experiences to endure. My childhood was painful when it came to being called sissy, fagot or gay. I grew up not ever feeling sure about who I was or what my purpose was. Time and time again I questioned God about my existence and asked why he made me go through such awful moments. I was in constant suffering about things no one else seemed to be bothered or worried about. To me, these things were a big deal. I took on the problems of my family and wore them on my shoulders night and day. I believed God made me different. I never truly felt a part of anything. I battled the hurtful comments concerning my being, my sexuality, my physicalness, my persona, and most importantly my manhood. But I became tired, even too tired to keep fighting the comments and the whispers behind my back. Even the chuckling and the innuendoes of so called friends and family became so normal; I became numb and unfeeling to all the scorn.

For a period in my life, I gave up and accepted the hurtful comments people made to me. I began believing what people said to me was true. It got so bad I would tell new faces and new friends they would not like me because of the things people thought about me. I had realized a self prophecy. The same one I fought against over and over, day in and day out with my father, sisters, bullies and schoolmates. I believed they were right about me. My self esteem was nonexistent. I had even, after the attack, reached a point where I no longer wanted to live; I wanted the pain to stop. I contemplated suicide to end the misery I felt. I began doing stupid things like getting drunk, smoking weed, selling drugs, and taking on risky tasks with the possibility of becoming injured. I just didn't flipping care anymore.

My summer in Scotland, CSA, Father, and my friends were the saving grace in my life. They were refreshing, especially CSA since it was my chance to realize my dreams of being an actor, and it allowed me to have the aspiration of a future and a whole new life. It was a crucial crossroad in my life. Fortunately, I lived through the rape, and it made me a stronger, more determined and focused man. I had almost given up. Had it not been for the blessings from above and the strength HE provided me, Lord knows what I would have done to myself.

I realized *after* the rape I never really thanked God for the blessings I received prior to the attack. It was only after the rape that I became grateful for all the enjoyable things I had done and experienced in my life. I was truly blessed and highly favored. God had his ways to compensate me for all the pain and suffering I was going through concerning my father and the situations with my family. I discovered that true happiness, success, and good fortune were the result of suffering a little and living through those sufferings while keeping faith in God. Accepting God's plans was difficult. I began thinking maybe hurtful times and suffering were prerequisites for receiving some type of tranquility of heart, peace of mind, and true and genuine joy.

It hurts me as a teacher to see some of my students go through similar experiences. I see it in their eyes; I can look into their hearts and see the hurt and pain they endure. I know some think my words of, "I know what you are going through," are oblivious to what is really happening in their lives. I do know what they are going through. How can I tell them it will be alright when I know good and well that there is a possibility things won't be alright? True, I made it. I was strong, and I had God. Some of my kids are lost. Some of them have nothing and nobody. I feel like such a hypocrite when I tell them things will be better. It takes something special to pull oneself out of a deep depression and sad state of mind. I do not know how I would have survived without God's grace and mercy over my life.

My students are worse off. There are more drugs, more alcohol, less parental involvement and less support from friends. I shiver to think of where some of my kids will end up. My commitment not only to empower them, but also to educate them about life itself and our roles in it have become paramount in my pedagogy. I try to inform my kids of the struggles they will face. I try to prepare their minds and wills to keep them focused and away from the evils of peers and the streets. I may reach some while others will be deaf to my words and advice. Hopefully, my reward from writing this book will be a student who knocks on my door ten years from now with a career and a success story to go along with it. I would like to feel as I made Mrs. Jones felt when I visited her after graduating from Ashland. She cried as she proudly rubbed my back. She needed to hear, "Thank You." It made her whole life, I think, I hope. I am certain it will make mine.

My perception of love suffered. I was girlfriend-less for a long, long time after the attack, and even when I began dating again, it was still extremely uncomfortable, awkward, and very, very different. I did not experience the same kind of feelings toward another human being since my trip to Scotland. And, although I've worked through the attack my own way, it has always affected me. Loving someone intimately was never the same. Trusting people in general continued to be extremely difficult for me.

Being raped made me a stronger person. It really did. I find myself not giving up so quickly. In difficult times or stressful situations, I encourage myself by thinking, "I've been through a lot worse than this and have made it." And most importantly, I find myself thanking the Lord for each and every day. I have learned to be grateful daily, for each and every morning I am allowed to wake up seeing, smelling, touching, feeling, and being me.

Chapter 10
"NOTHING COMES TO SLEEPERS, BUT A DREAM"

Class of 1988

Graduation and prom came so fast. It was like the entire year had whisked by in the blink of an eye. The class attempted to preserve its unity as much as it could by continuously getting together at each others' houses on the weekends and after school or simply planning activities together. Since we enjoyed each other's company, we remain connected. The week of graduation, we had a senior cut day where went to the movie theater; the beach, Cedar Point, and to the zoo. It was so much fun! We were such a close class. So close that the rest of the school resented us at times. We became known as 88 The Great!

I suspect most people couldn't stand our class because of our solidarity. We were like a family of brothers and sisters. Don't get me wrong, now; there were difficult times, but we always managed to talk things out and work through our arguments and misunderstandings. That's just the type of class we were. Our solidarity showed many times through protest.

We led a walk-out in the winter of senior year. The school building was ice cold because the school boiler could not be turned on until a certain date. According to our principal, "Winter had not officially started." Everyone complained about the cold. It was unbelievably frigid in all of our classrooms.

Talking seemed to get us no heat, or asking teachers to complain on our behalf. The cold led me to stand in the hallway and yell, "Walk Out!" during a midmorning class exchange. The seniors, juniors, and some sophomores, walked out and went home. The principal received an enormous amount of calls since kids were arriving home early in the day. The parents demanded the heat be turned on. The following day CSA was warm! I was called to the office and given a lecture on how to go about getting something without having to cause disruptions. I responded by expressing how things didn't get done until someone stood up for what was right. It was then I was indirectly told I would be suspended if I ever led another school-wide disruption.

Our class made our school popular. We provided CSA with a spirit it had never possessed. We created an atmosphere of such pride that we were the talk of our district. CSA was disliked by many schools for its popularity. Our kids constantly appeared on T.V, in the paper, and even on the radio. John Hay and the other high schools constantly made fun of our students, especially the boys. I imagine "boys in tights" was not readily acceptable. But it wasn't just the dance majors; the music and theater majors were constantly harassed as well on morning commutes to school on public transportation. I guess to the other schools, "real" boys played football or basketball.

CSA's reputation was due to 88 and its seniors. CSA's musical production of Peter Pan at the State Theater was outstanding. The media credited our production as worthy enough to be on Broadway. We couldn't help being the best in the city not only in the performing arts, but also in boys' volleyball, girls' basketball, cheerleading, attendance, and high test scores on the Ohio Proficiency Test. Our school was continuously acknowledged and noted for its fabulous work as well as the tenacity of its children when it came to speaking out publicly about the disastrous and horrible conditions of the building.

Our class was notorious when it came to standing up for something which seemed unfair. We never let down a fight. I remember the day the workers came out to plaster some of the walls and ceilings. The media credited the senior class for the attention the building received due to the speech and the protest of the students at the monthly school board meeting. Several teachers congratulated me for being active and standing up to the administration. Although I spear headed most of the gripes and petitions, it was the enormous support of my class that made things happen. When I visit CSA today, some of my former teachers tell me there hasn't been a class like ours since we graduated. That makes me feel both good and sad.

Our administration did nothing to find another location for our graduation. It was probably their way of getting back at us for all the commotion we had caused. Our principal didn't like us because of all the attention we had drawn to the school. But had the waves not been created, many of the issues would have been kept on the back burner as usual. Needless to say, I was not crazy about the principal as I am sure he was not too crazy about me. Although at graduation, he pulled me over to the side and stated I would always be one of his favorite adversaries.

Our year ended with the chase. The day before graduation, we were chased across the street following commencement rehearsal in the John Hay auditorium. A group of John Hay students ran after us across the street into our parking lot as they threw bricks and tree branches at us. I guess they weren't too happy about our commencement taking place in their school. On the big day, we must have had what seemed to be the entire police department at graduation. What a shame it was. Graduation was marred with all the police officers. After it was over, we had one last get together in the parking lot where we embraced, cried and said farewell to one another. It was a bitter departure to a class which truly left a legacy at CSA.

And that was how my high school years came to a close. What a journey. And how fitting, I thought, was the word commencement. Our last hugs, and tears, in that dusty parking lot, meant the beginning of a whole new life. From Jefferson, to Broadriver, Marvin, Case, The Mac, Willson, and CSA. What a remarkable and unforgettable journey. As exciting as it was that night, emotions of sadness and fear crept into my being. A brief moment had whisked by in my mind where I asked myself was I ready to take on the world and move forward into life? I reached a point in my life where it meant no longer being babied and stood over. It was the end of teachers and schools and the beginning of adulthood!

Chapter 11
THE LAST SUMMER

This was it, my last summer as a young man. From here on, it was work, work, and more work. It was made very clear to look for a job and help pay some of the household bills. Although I worked, I did manage to enjoy my last summer as a young adult. I spent the summer of '88 with Michelle and Carlos. Omari and I stopped talking. He went his way and I went mine.

Omari didn't attend CSA his Senior year; he went to John Adams to play football. I think it was for the better. It would have been very hard to be around him senior year after the attack. It all worked out for the best, even though our friendship totally faded away. Up to that point in my life, I considered Omari a genuine friend, like Michelle and Tyrone. He had been the only other close male friend since Tyrone, and that was almost five years prior. We surely experienced a hell of a lot. What happened to our relationship made me feel even more down in the dumps and depressed, but again I dealt with it, as hard as it was.

Carlos

Carlos had come at a perfect time. We knew each other through volleyball. CSA and Collinwood High School played each other during volleyball season. He was also kind of related to me through my niece. But even though we weren't really family, we called each other cousins. We favored somewhat in looks, so what the heck. Besides, everywhere we went, people would ask us if we were brothers. After a while, we agreed to tell people we were cousins.

Our friendship began when we saw each other at a party and exchanged phone numbers. We began hanging out. First, it was him and me. Then, it was Michelle, Carlos and I. We became the best of friends. We spent most of our time at the beach. We'd sit on the rocks and talk for hours. Most of the conversations were centered on our future plans, goals, and aspirations. Carlos had decided to go to the Army. Michelle and I were going off to college.

Although we had good times that summer, I couldn't help but think how sad I would be in college without my friends. Leaving Willson to go to CSA was different. I was eager to start over and forget about junior high. But with college, I didn't want to leave my friends from high school. My biggest fear was going to a college, a white private college, and not having anything in common with the people there. I had become so accustomed to being around my friends, my Black friends, that I think I became color struck. I realized at that point I didn't have white friends whatsoever. The only white associates I had were those in the "Look Up To Cleveland" group. They were okay, even though at times it was difficult making small talk.

Carlos became my best friend. It seemed Carlos and I became joined at the hip. We were inseparable. Everywhere he was, I was. Everywhere I went, he went. When it was time for him to go to the Army, I became very, very, depressed. I hit rock bottom and started to drink. Days after his departure, I went to the beach to visit our old hang out place and drink on the rocks by myself. Getting geeked was my way of escaping the feeling of aloneness. Being plastered was the only way to forget about being depressed. I can't even begin to tell all the times I drunk by myself into a stupor. Now, when I think about those times, I think how stupid! I was so angry at the world and so full of self pity. I thank God I didn't become an alcoholic like my father.

The depression came from not having my CSA friends around anymore. It seemed to me like my connections with them were fading away after graduation. Maybe the only fabric keeping us together was CSA. Now that we were no longer in school, it was hard to accept people were moving on in separate paths. Why was it so difficult for me to do the same? Move on? Begin a new chapter? I questioned myself constantly, wondering if it was something I was doing or not doing? Was it embarrassing to have me for a friend? I began to think it was my fault. I felt just as I did in elementary and junior high when the kids used to call me out my name. I remember how no one, especially the boys, wanted to be around me or befriend me for fear of what others might think. I felt like I had a plague. A sickness that keeps people away.

Would I have this problem in college? This was one of the reasons for not being at all enthused about going off to college. I felt so alone after Carlos left because next to Tyrone, Michelle and Omari, Carlos accepted me for me; he was the closest friend I had. Being depressed made me have a "who cares" attitude. I just wanted to drink myself into oblivion. I started smoking cigarettes, and on occasions, marijuana. I even started selling drugs.

Slanging

I went from being very sad and depressed to being very mean and angry. My "who gives a crap" attitude made me bitter. I just didn't care what happened to me. I managed to make a few contacts with some associates from Willson, and before I knew it I was making weed drops. It kills me to rehash this brief chapter because I was so stupid to have done such a thing. I can't believe I was such an idiot.

It started off with small portions, I guess as a kind of a trial basis, and although I made good money, the problem was dealing with my conscience. It was killing me. This was something I was totally against. I can't even begin to explain why...Why did I allow myself to be a runner? Being depressed and so mad at the world can make you do stupid, stupid things.

I just didn't care. I was tired of working and making so little. I wanted quick money, fast money, like everyone else. Thank God I ended it. I made about three hundred dollars the first week, but the fear of being caught outweighed the money I made. And the man I was running for wasn't the nicest person in the world; he frightened me. I did not trust him. And being his runner was not simple. It was anxiety filled, scary and humiliating.

It was demeaning and it felt like slave work. "Do this, do that, run this here, run this there…" it was too much to handle. I had to find a way to get out. I was terrified for my life. I knew it would be difficult cutting loose. I told the man I was going away to college. He asked no questions. He dapped me up, nodded his head, and waited for me to leave. After two weeks, it was over, and I was relieved to be alive and out of jail!

As I recall this episode in my life, all I can think was I must have completely lost my almighty mind! It was the anger that drove me to do something so risky, dangerous, and stupid. I was extremely angry with Omari, Carlos, and Michelle. Feeling so alone and abandoned, I didn't give a crap what happened to me.

The evil one knew and took advantage of it. Every bit of it!

I called Omari after Michelle and Carlos were gone. I wanted to talk and get things straightened out, but it was too late! Omari had enlisted in the Marines; he too was gone.

I was a total mess. Feeling alone and highly depressed, I wanted to crawl away and die. I felt just as I did after being whipped by my father, being called names at school, when I was attacked, and when I graduated from school. Alone!

Thank God almighty that Father was still in my life. My friendship with him became stronger and closer. He was my rock and my council. Father saved me from totally losing it. He always managed to say something that would put life into a different perspective. I could always count on Father to look at the bright side of what seemed to be the most awful situation. He taught me to always look for the good in something no matter how horrible it was or seemed. I'll never forget what he said once: "When a door slams shut on you, the Lord will open a window." Had it not been for his constant support, I would have ended up in a heap of trouble.

I kept my mind off the things that depressed me and stayed away from the house by picking up the third shift at McDonald's on the turnpike. I would even volunteer regularly to work double shifts. I needed the money for college, and besides, it was my excuse for being out of the house. Working especially helped me to forget how bad I really felt about Michelle going off to college, Carlos going to the Army, and Omari going to the Marines. I can't begin to express how dreadful it was to feel like there wasn't a soul in the world who understood what I was going through. It seemed like I was totally and completely alone as far as friends, true, and genuine friends were concerned. It was, without a doubt, the most horrible feeling in the world. I kept myself busy with work and volleyball. It was the only way to keep from being so sad about my friends and all the problems in the family. Being alone was hard.

The one good thing that came from all this pain was my relationship with the Lord. I became even closer to God since I spent most of the time having internal conversations with him. I'd ask him to bless me with a little happiness and relieve me and my family from so many problems.

As if it wasn't bad enough dealing with this identity thing, I was also feeling the trauma of my older sister, her new baby, and my mom. Gladys and Mom were having so many problems which again, affected me to the core.

At the time Gladys, was raising my niece by herself and was, without saying, struggling enormously. Gladys was in and out of the house and in and out of our lives. She and Mom would get into it about something, and Gladys would pack her things and leave. Mom was so disappointed and angry with Gladys after her pregnancy, that all they did was fight and argue. I use the words fight and argue loosely since most of their confrontations I remember being so nasty. My father was an S.O.B., but Mom was no joke either. She had her moments when she'd blow her top. And when she did, it wasn't pretty.

Most of the fights before the pregnancy were because Gladys was not following the house rules about curfew or about who she was hanging around with. Mom blamed Gladys's friends for what happened to her with the girls that beat her up in front of the house. She warned Gladys constantly about who she chose for friends. She told Gladys her so-called friends were going to get her into trouble. When Gladys told Mom she was pregnant, Mom immediately blamed it on her "no good friends." Mom was beside herself. She could not believe Gladys had gotten pregnant after all the warnings, lectures, and talks. It was embarrassing for Mom but most of all disappointing.

Ulcer?

She and Gladys fought so much it made me have dreadful stomach and headaches to the point where I did not want to eat. When I did eat, food burned my insides, and I'd get the urge to vomit. My eating habits were completely out of whack. The only time I'd eat was when I got terribly hungry...extremely hungry. The urge to be full was never there because I knew if I ate, I would heave. There was nothing worse than feeling nauseated; I hated it. I never went to see a doctor, but I believe I had an ulcer. Food burned my insides. It was like eating fire. I remember the pain above my belly button. I'd press the spot as hard as I could to sooth the pain. Sometimes, it worked; others, it wouldn't and continued to burn.

It became difficult to hide the pain, especially if we were all having dinner together. Having excuses for not eating became a great task. I was amazed at myself for always making up a new excuse each time I didn't eat at home. The two that worked the best were, "I ate at the rectory with Father," or, "I had a big lunch at school." Needless to say, I had to come up with other excuses, especially during the weekends and on vacations from school. It helped to have a job because then I could say I ate at McDonald's or something.

Mom put Gladys into a home for young pregnant mothers. It tore me up because I could tell Gladys was dejected. She looked so sad. My father became worse. He drank and drank, which only added more wood to the already heated fire. Alina was still young, but I could tell it affected her since she and Gladys were so close. With me, I just cried at night, asking God to fix everything and make things better. It was hard every time Gladys left because after the baby, Adriana, was born, I become very attached to her, especially after we almost lost her.

Adriana was born colic. To this day, I still believe it was all the stress Gladys went through while she was pregnant. She was a senior in a Catholic high school and had to deal with all the pressures of her teachers and classmates. Imagine being pregnant in an all girls' Catholic high school... it wasn't something people were used to seeing, and it caused Gladys a lot of ridicule. I was convinced all the stress was harmful to the baby during her pregnancy which caused Adriana's eating difficulties.

After Adriana was born, she constantly cried and cried, and it was very difficult to feed her. It seemed like she did not want to drink her bottles of milk. About a month after she was born, Adriana almost choked to death. Gladys fed her a bottle of formula and laid her in the bassinet when moments later, we heard her coughing. She had spit up and was choking on her vomit. I remember the yell Gladys let out when she went into the room and found Adriana red as a tomato; it sent such a horrifying and cold feeling through my body.

Adriana was turning colors. We called the ambulance as Mom and Gladys attempted to help her breathe. Mom ran with her to the next door neighbor. Our neighbor grabbed Adriana, and with a strong breath blew in her face. Adriana let out the vomit she had in her throat and began to cry. I remember thinking how wonderful it was to hear her cry. The ambulance arrived moments later. They made sure she was okay and went off. It was the most frightful feeling I had ever felt. When I knew she was going to be okay, I fell on my knees. With the rosary in my hand, I began yelling, "Thank you God, Thank you God." I just cried and cried tears of relief and joy. "Thank you God, thank you, thank you, thank you."

Mom became withdrawn from all of us after the baby was born. She became very stern, hard, and introverted. She didn't smile, or laugh, or joke around anymore. She turned into a whole different person. I imagine the move to Cleveland, the living conditions, the lack of finances, being on welfare, the accident, my father's drinking and not working, the lawsuit, and Gladys's pregnancy was enough to make her evolve into such a mean person. But I could not blame her. Mom thought we blamed her for all the problems. I never understood why she thought that. I never remember blaming her for anything. But I understood her pain, and it seemed I was the only one that did. The rest of the family couldn't deal with Mom's new attitude; they would argue, and argue and argue with Mom. My home and my insides were in complete mayhem. All I could do was continue to pray for a little bit of peace of mind.

The week of college orientation I was so down and so sick. I ended up in the hospital for three days with a high fever and a stomach virus. To this day, I'm convinced my depression gave me that fever and virus. All I could remember as I sat in the hospital was how miserable I would be going to an all white private college. I felt guilty going off to school. How could I leave Mom? I'd be leaving her to the wolves if I went off to college. She wouldn't have any one on her side. She'd be all alone to defend herself. Guilt, guilt, guilt. Damn! What to do? There was nothing I could do. I had to go; I needed to get away. I heard God's voice telling me, "This is your time and your turn".

Chapter 12
COLLEGE FRESHMEN

    The summer of "88 seemed like only two weeks long. I was packing my things to leave before I knew it. The ride down to Ashland was eternal. Mom talked me to death the entire way about eating well, washing clothes correctly, and being in bed at a descent hour. She was simply doing the "mom" thing, and was probably more nervous than I was. That was the impression I got. My father didn't say very much. I really don't think he understood the concept of "going off" to college since he continued to ask if I would be home in a couple of days. I tried to tell him I was going to live on campus, but he persisted to ask when I'd be coming home. Finally, after a while I replied, "Este fin de semana" (this weekend).

    It didn't hit me right away that my father was showing some emotion toward me. Was he so concerned about when I'd be coming home because maybe he was going to miss me? "Oh, my," I thought. Was my father expressing a little sorrow once he realized I was not going back with the family? I was overwhelmed with shock. I became numb! I couldn't react. I don't think, at the time, I knew how to react to my father's suddenly missing me.

My roommate's name was Jeff. He was a White kid from a small rural town in Ohio. Jeff was very nice and very friendly. My sister, Alina, and my mom fell in love with him. The last thing Mom said to Jeff was, "Take care of my son." Jeff smiled and replied, "I will. Don't worry." I knew Jeff and I would be okay.

Everything was fine up to the point of saying goodbye. After my things were unpacked and Mom put everything, and I mean everything, in its place, my father decided it was time to leave. Everyone had come for the ride; my parents, two sisters, niece, and my oldest sister's new boyfriend who drove the other car. I didn't think I would lose it like I did since I was ready for them to leave; I was excited about walking around campus with Jeff.

Alina and Gladys said goodbye first, then my father. He embraced me, gave me a kiss on the forehead and said "Cuidate mi hijo" (take care my son). Mom's hug made me cry. She whispered in my ear, "Estudie mucho (study a lot), not too much television, and lots of rest." I completely lost it when it was my niece's turn to say goodbye. She didn't want to leave the room until she was sure I was going back with them. Not only did my father not understand about my staying, my niece didn't either. When she realized I wasn't going back with them, she went crazy. She completely had a fit. Her eyes swelled with tears as she cried out, "Vente tio, vente tio," (come on uncle). I tried to console her by telling her I would see her in a couple of days, even though I was not telling the truth. She asked, "Promise tio (uncle)?" I nodded yes. I couldn't bring myself to tell her I would not be seeing her until Thanksgiving break. As they drove away, Jeff left me alone. He could see I was upset. I sobbed as I watched Mom and Adriana's little hand waving bye bye to me. The only thing I could feel and think was, "Oh My God, I'm on my own, I'm really on my own!"

It was difficult getting used to having a new life, a new roommate and new friends. My first semester in college was very challenging. It was the "make or break" phase in my college life. I never imagined I would be dealing with people who had little to no experience with other races or ethnic backgrounds. I will never forget the hurdles I overcame my first semester with the guys on the floor and with Jeff.

The night of the first floor meeting, one of the very first questions directed at me was, "What are you?" I knew then I would be dealing with a lot of ignorant people. The guys on the floor had very little contact with Blacks or Latinos if any. Most of the guys expressed they came from majority White schools. They explained there were Black students in their high schools but never more than a handful. I gathered the guys had very little knowledge and experiences with ethnic people in general. I explained to them I was raised in an all Black neighborhood, went to a predominantly all Black high school, and had only Black friends. I wanted them to understand that college was a new experience for me too, as far as being around White people was concerned. Most of the guys agreed it was also a new experience for them being around a Latino from the inner city.

The guy who asked me the question expressed he was confused. "You don't look White, and you don't look Black, but you sound Black." Immediately, I remembered the time I left Case to go to The Mac. I assumed the street accent, dialect or whatever you want to call it, and the fact that I only listened to rap and hip hop was the reason for his asking me, "What are you?" Some thought I was a light skinned Black; others assumed I was mixed; the majority assumed I was Puerto Rican. After telling them I was Colombian, one of the boys asked, "Isn't Colombian the same thing as Puerto Rican?" I thought, "Oh Lord, this is going to be quite interesting."

Music was the main way I met new faces and made new acquaintances. When I played my music, different people would come to my room to ask about the group or artist I was listening to. Most of the guys on the floor were very accepting, but there were a few who wanted nothing to do with me. It was made very clear who they were, especially when I'd listen to my music and leave the door of the room open. I'd hear some of the doors slam shut. Some would blare their own music, most of which was hard rock, to drown out my music with their own.

Jeff and I were fine up until he started pledging a fraternity. The majority of our disagreements were in regards to my space, food, and my bed. It seemed like every time his pledge brothers came to the room, they plopped themselves on my bed. Jeff conveniently had a loft, so he did not have that problem. I explained to Jeff I did not appreciate having folks sit in the same place where I lay my face and body at night. It was beyond me why he could not comprehend my vexation about the bed. The other problem was simple. I asked Jeff to inform his friends that my cupboards and refrigerator was not a public supermarket. Every time he had company, something of mine would be gone or eaten. The bed wasn't as big of a deal as my food. I made it quite clear not to mess with my darn food.

Because of his pledging and his fraternity brothers, Jeff and I grew further apart. He was constantly being awakened in the middle of the night, and his ongoing company was affecting my studying. I explained to Jeff it was okay if he wanted to flunk out and ruin his college career, but I refused for him to be the cause of me getting bad grades due to a lack of rest. I made him aware of my struggle to be in college and assured him I was not going to allow him or any other person to hinder me from achieving my goal...earning a degree!

I wanted to get good grades my first semester. That was my ultimate goal. I was very serious about my classes and very serious about my quiet time for studying and reading. Jeff's pledging was affecting all those things, and I didn't like it one bit. Since he and his pledge brothers continued their lack of respect when it concerned me, my space and my things, I had to do what was best for me and that was leave. I told Jeff I would be moving out at the end of the semester even though I wanted to leave sooner. I didn't let the door incident run me out of the dorm.

"Nigger Lover"

The door incident was my first experience with racism and prejudice at Ashland. One day, when I returned from class I noticed something odd about the door to my room. It had white foamy stuff on it. I initially thought it was a prank since during the week someone was putting Vaseline and shaving cream on all the doorknobs. When I reached the door, I noticed the shaving cream was someone's message to me which read, "NIGGER LOVER." I was incensed! My insides went completely cold. I was astonished and very angry!

My first intention was to go off! I wanted to go to the room that always played the rock when my music was on. I was almost positive it was them who wrote those words on my door. They were three boys who shared a room down the hallway. The same three who always made comments or had things to say about my music. After trying to calm down, I stopped myself and thought, "I have no proof it was them. This is what these ignorant bastards want; to make me angry, loose my cool, and have me fight and be kicked out of college." I decided I was not going to allow someone to push my buttons and have that satisfaction and power over me. My revenge would be saying things out loud as I cleaned the door. "It's too bad ignorant mutha****** act like little boys and not men on this floor. A real man would handle his problems face to face, and not hide behind a bottle of shaving cream." I knew everyone would hear me since by now the entire floor heard about what happened and everyone was standing outside their doors. I could tell by the look on a few faces they didn't like the comment. But what could they have done? Nothing! Had anybody said something back to me, it would have been clear who wrote the message on my door. The person or persons who did it never came forward nor did anyone ever tell me who did it. My only vengeance was knowing that someone was rubbed the wrong way about the comments I made during my tirade.

There were other incidents like the sounds of beat boxing behind my back as I walked down the hallways, the evenings when I'd lie in bed as individuals would run past my door screaming, "Arriba, Arriba, Ándale, Ándale," and the continuous remarks concerning the people I hung around with. I'd lay in bed night after night asking God to give me patience and the strength to keep calm and not give in to the taunting and the discriminatory remarks. Believe me when I say there were moments when I felt pushed a little too much, but I managed to get through those difficult times by praying and having faith things would get better.

Sometimes, I'd call Mom angry and upset. There were several times I called to tell her I couldn't take it anymore. I was coming home. She would say "Reze mi hijo, reze" (pray my son, pray). Just hearing her voice made me feel better.

In all my life, I never felt so much stress when it came to race and friendships. It was beyond me why so many people had a problem with who I hung around with, the way I talked, or the music I listened to. I guess to the Whites I was a "wanna be" or a "whiger" as they put it. (Later I deciphered that a "whiger" was the name Whites used to describe other Whites who acted or wanted to be Black. A White Nigger, if you will.) Although I wasn't White and didn't consider myself to be White, the term "whiger" still bothered me.

Most of the friends I made *were* Black. I felt accepted by the brothers and sisters I had met. I *was* accepted. Period! I felt more comfortable being around my Black friends than my White friends.

Black was what I was used to, who I grew up with, who I went to school with; it was the only thing I knew. Besides, I never felt questioned or out of place like those times when I'd be around the White students. It's hard to explain. I wanted to have all types of friends, not just Black friends, but the White students didn't make it easy. I was constantly being questioned about the way I talked, who I hung around with and what music I listened to. There weren't many Blacks at Ashland, and to my knowledge, I was the only Latino on the yard at the time. If there were any other Latinos, I never met them. To me, it wasn't a matter of Black or White. I simply wanted to feel comfortable with having new friends. Because Blacks and Latinos have always, throughout History and modern times, shared more commonalities than shades of differences in our appearance, cultures, traditions, likes, dislikes, struggles and even prejudices, I felt more a part of the Black population on the yard. Nevertheless, my choice of friends always seemed to be a big issue, especially when it came to one of my majors...theater.

Theatre

I went to Ashland to earn a degree in Theater Education. My objective was to one day be Mr. Fisher from CSA. The School of the Arts had a tremendous impact on my life and future. I wanted to be to others what my teachers were to me, an inspiration, a role model, a guide to a successful life. My ultimate goal was to go back and teach in Cleveland.

Because I was on a theater scholarship, I had to perform or work all of the productions in the department whether through acting or technical work. I was the only person of color in the entire department. Talk about racial tension! Being a theater major was hell at times. Life was not easy, especially when it came time to audition for the productions. Needless to say, I was typecast into every role of every play I auditioned for.

My first role was a poker player in the play, A Street Car Named Desire. The role, if I'm not mistaken, was a character called Pablo. The second role was my very first lead role. I played the rapist, Raul, in the play Extremities. My third and final role of freshman year was a rapist in the musical Man of La Mancha. It was quite clear what my future was going to be as far as theater was concerned. The theater department became my worst adversaries.

It was a daily battle dealing with innuendoes, indirect remarks, whom I portrayed myself to be, and who I befriended. It was a tug a war when it came to hanging out. The theater majors tried their hardest to convert and recruit me into the theater click. But the more they insisted, the more I was turned off. I wasn't fond of the philosophy behind the theater click. They wanted it to be just them and no one else. I wanted to be free to hang out with whomever I wanted...not just the theater people. I wanted to be able to have more friends than just the theater majors. My decision to be my own person was costly. Life was made miserable for me when it came to theater. I hated feeling like I had to make a choice between one or the other. In the end, I chose to be with the group I felt most at home with, the brothers and the sisters. In fact, I ended up feeling nothing but resentment toward the department for putting me in a position where I was made to feel like I had to choose.

  The majority of the Blacks on the yard (campus) were either on the track, basketball, or football teams. It wasn't long before I realized that the majority of the Blacks at Ashland were there for a sport. I don't know why that made me feel awkward, even rubbed me the wrong way. I just knew that it bothered me. I asked myself, if there weren't any sports, would there be any Black students at Ashland? Maybe it was just me, but I'd bet a million dollars there wouldn't have been. It concerned me to realize that in life, the only way for some people to go to college was through their ability to score touchdowns, shoot three pointers or run races. At times, I felt as though the university did back flips to recruit Black athletes but did very little to recruit people of color for their good grades and mental capacities. Maybe I was crazy. Nonetheless, that was the way I perceived the minority enrollment at Ashland to be.

"The Ghetto"

It was quite evident how many people of color attended the university, especially during meals. The Blacks sat together in an isolated part of the cafeteria named "The Ghetto." I can't remember why it was called the ghetto. I do remember the term being used in a conversation in the theater lounge. When I asked who named it the ghetto, someone responded, "Isn't it obvious?" It was then I was asked why I sat in the ghetto. I didn't mind eating in the ghetto since the majority of my friends were Black. I enjoyed eating there! It made me feel at home.

Was I purposely not sitting with the Whites? Were the Blacks trying to make a statement by sitting together? I don't think so. It was the only time we had to be together as a group of friends and as a people. It is my conclusion that the ghetto was a place where alike people ate together. That's all, nothing else! The Blacks were no different from all the fraternities, sororities, and exchange groups which sat together to eat. While it was always a topic of, "The Blacks isolating themselves from the Whites," there wasn't ever an initiative by the Whites to sit in the ghetto or intertwine and mingle with the Blacks. People were so busy making an issue of the Blacks segregating themselves on purpose, that no one ever cared to think that the majority of the population which sat together were in fact the Whites on the yard. It was simply easier to see the division with the Blacks because of the difference in skin color.

It was interesting now that I think about it because no one ever made an issue about any other group, or click sitting together. The talk was always, or seemed always to be about the Blacks and "the ghetto." The ghetto was a place that reminded me of high school. It was a place to relax and share thoughts, feelings, stories and other things between classes. It was a place to let go of frustrations. It was the only location on the entire yard where unity and family was evident among the Blacks. Maybe the Whites had a problem with the ghetto not because of the isolation factor, but, and I might be right in saying this, maybe they just could not stand to see how close the Blacks were and how close we stuck together. Maybe that was the real problem people had with the ghetto; the bonding!

Chapter 13
ACADEMICS

My classes were not at all too difficult. They were challenging but not to the point where I couldn't handle them. The major factors in regards to academia was disciplining myself to read the assignments and have homework and papers completed on time. College meant being free from parental and teacher control. In high school, teachers made an effort to remind me of assignments and deadlines. College was different. On the first day of each class, I was given a syllabus with assignments and due dates. That was it! It was clear the professors were not going to hound me for work or be on my back to have things turned in on time. It scared me because I was very undisciplined as far as studying and work was concerned. I needed someone to be on my butt in order to produce good work. I think the hardest part of college was getting used to getting down to business.

The key was self motivation. I had to learn how to self discipline myself and create study habits that worked effectively for me. I would have to say that the most difficult thing to do was to sit and read. Since elementary school, I have always had difficulties understanding concepts the first time around. I found myself reading assignments two and three times over and over. It was time consuming and very frustrating. It reminded me of my first year at The Mac.

As a college student, I realized I was fortunate to have had the training of a private school at an early age. It was a good solid foundation for knowing how to read and do assignments. I recalled the strategies I learned at The Mac about reading and summarizing. Of course back then, I was not allowed to write in the text books; I had to write on separate sheets of paper. Since the books in college were mine, I was able to write my summaries right on the pages. I felt fortunate to have been taught how to summarize and paraphrase material I read. It was the key to understanding what I was reading. It became my saving grace in college.

Other unforgettable strategies were the ones I learned at CSA. Paraphrasing class lectures and writing essays. Boy, did these come in handy! I have to give credit to Mr. Steinmetz and Dr. Murphy from CSA. They were the ones who taught me how to write papers correctly; write what you are going to say , write it, write what you've just said. At first, I was writing everything the professors were saying. It took time to re-teach myself how and what to write in my notebooks. It was such a helpful technique and so simple but so very important. Had it not been for them, writing papers would have been torture for me.

Stupid?

The first couple of months were very trying. Not only was I dealing with stress in the dorm, but also in the classroom. I understood the ignorance of the guys on the floor, but never expected to get the same from certain professors. I was stunned when two of my professors suggested I take the hundred courses in English and Math. At the time, I didn't know what hundred courses entailed. I didn't understand why I was being asked to take them. I wasn't even given a chance to do the first couple of assignments to see whether or not I needed to take the remedial courses. I do recall, the first few days of classes, being asked what school system I came from. When I told both professors that I was a product of the Cleveland Public Schools, it was then when it was indirectly suggested to me I take the remedial courses. Both professors, in two different classes! I couldn't believe it. I didn't know what to think. I felt so belittled. I thought it was one of two things; they were either concerned and wanted to help me, or they had prejudged me as a failure. It was odd to me that both professors in both classes asked only me. Later, I realized I was the only person from the Cleveland Public School System in both of the classes. When I questioned the two professors respectively, both responses were similar, "I think it will be beneficial for you to take the hundred courses before you take my class." Since I wasn't suffering from trauma to the brain, nor did I need a ton of bricks to fall on my head, it was loud and clear what had happened. The two professors had come to the conclusion that... Latino + Cleveland Public Schools = Stupid.

I asked around about the hundred courses. To my dismay, I found out they were courses offered to students who came to college with poor grades and in need of remediation. Around the yard, the hundred courses were known as "dummy Math and dummy English." I also discovered the credits did not count toward graduation. I was boiling, but determined! I had made up my mind there was no way I was going to let this pass. I vowed to show them! And just how was I going to do it? The best way was with my first report card.

I made it a point to prove to the two professors I could handle their work...anybody's work, anybody's class! I worked my behind off in and out of all my classes. I always made sure to ask questions and solicit help when I needed it. Most of the help came from the college's writing center. Not only did the center help me in my studies, but it also gave me the opportunity to work with computers. The writing center became my favorite place to study and to go for help.

My G.P.A. after first semester was a 3.8. I earned straight A's and two A-'s. My mission was accomplished! It felt so good. More than good. I felt empowered!

Now, as I look back, I am grateful for what those two professors did to me. Had it not been for their ignorance, I would have never realized my potential and capabilities to do whatever I set my mind on. It was after receiving my first report card that I discovered my destiny, my future, and my life was totally in my own hands. I was the only Latino on the entire yard, on the Dean's list, and with a 3.8 grade point average! It was absolutely...Fantástico!

Second semester, I moved to a different dorm with a friend I made from Shaker Heights. His name was Chaz. Chaz and I became friends when I tried out for the track team. Even though I did not stay on the team, he and I remained friends. We decided to get a room since the both of us had bad luck with our roommates in the fall.

It was a totally new environment. The building had more of a college atmosphere since it was situated in the heart of the campus. I could see the other dorms and most of the classroom buildings from my window. In the mornings, I enjoyed watching the change of classes. All the students would come out of the buildings at once, and it made me feel as if I was in a big university. I felt proud and important to be a part of college life. Who would have ever thought that I would be in college? Who would have ever thought that a Latino from the inner city "barrio" would be studying at a private and expensive institution? I beat all the odds and proved not only to myself, but to others who doubted me, that it was possible to go to college. All it took was a focused head and determination. I felt extremely fortunate to be in college. I almost could not believe it. For a while, it just didn't seem real.

Ashland was not a university my freshman year; it was called Ashland College. It changed its name my sophomore year to Ashland University. I assumed the change from college to university was supposed to attract more students. But there were other reasons; the increase in enrollment and being the only division two school in the state of Ohio. I just remember purchasing school Paraphernalia freshmen year so that one day I could say I attended Ashland when it was Ashland College. I know...big deal.

Freshman year, the enrollment was about three thousand with commuters. Approximately two thousand lived on campus. As the years went by, more students came to Ashland. The Black population also increased, and again, most were athletes. Interestingly, those that weren't athletes were female Blacks. Still no Latinos. There were students from other countries in the exchange program, but as far as regular students from the states who were Latino…….none. Again, if there were, I never meet them. Ashland was small enough that it was possible to either know everyone or know of everyone. And because of theater productions I participated in, I was well known.

Most of the athletes and Blacks lived in the building I moved into. Chaz was from my hometown, and I felt more comfortable than the first dorm. I expected things to go more smoothly since Chaz and I had the same friends, and we basically liked the same things like music. Chaz did have a problem though. I discovered later he was a third year student with sophomore status. This meant one of two things; either he was a transfer student and Ashland didn't accept all his credits, or he was one of those students who made going to college a profession. Unfortunately, it turned out to be number two.

I later discovered, to my dismay, Chaz was a tyrant for not attending class. He stayed out all night and slept in what seemed to be every morning. The only thing I kept thinking was, "Oh my God, what did I get myself into?" While I lived with him, I never saw him with a book or book bag. It was beyond my comprehension what he was doing. I never asked because I simply wanted to avoid a discussion or argument. Besides, it was none of my business. So long as my study time and space was not violated or disrespected, I didn't give a rat's behind what he did. It wasn't until the parties and the lack of sleep that I decided once again, it was time to move on. I moved out one Friday afternoon about a month into the semester.

The Monday of that week, Chaz invited several of his lady friends from Cleveland to come up for the entire week. He neglected to inform me they'd be staying the week in our room. Without say, I was not at all pleased. It became very uptight, especially in the evenings, and early mornings. After two of the girls dropped their things off in the room, I never saw them again until Friday afternoon. Apparently, the two found somewhere to stay for the week. Later, I discovered that the two had stayed with some football players in the dorm.

The third girl stayed with Chaz and me. Let's just say that the old saying, "A third wheel," more than applied to how I felt and what the entire week had amounted to. He never mentioned her while we were roommates nor did he ever tell me he had a girlfriend. Later, I was told they weren't girlfriend-boyfriend; they were close friends, really close friends! Let's just say she and Chaz woke me up on several occasions in the middle of the night during her stay.

I was awoken by the sounds of Chaz and her having sex. I couldn't believe it the first time it happened. But there they were, naked. As I lay still not knowing what to do, I was chagrined and very embarrassed. I found myself turning over in the bed with the pillow wrapped around my head trying to block out the noise. They went at it every night the entire week. I was to the point where I wanted to throw them out, but of course I couldn't since it was not just my room. The worst part about the week was on that Thursday when I came in from one of my classes, I opened the door and found them performing oral sex. I was frozen in the doorway. I just stood there in complete shock. They didn't seem to mind at all. It was as if nothing ever happened. She simply got up, turned her back to me, and began fixing her hair. Chaz didn't seem to mind at all since all he said was, "Didn't you have a class? My bad, man." I didn't say anything. I put my books on my bed and walked out of the room. I must have been three shades of red. That's how my face felt anyway. I figured they would be finished in an hour, so I just left. When I came back an hour later, she and Chaz weren't done at all. In fact, they were having sexual intercourse on the floor. Chaz saw that I'd opened the door but she didn't. I don't think she heard the door open due to all her moaning and screaming. Chaz turned around and smirked at me as he gestured for me to leave. I was so aggravated that I immediately went to the resident assistant and asked if I could move into the empty room down the hallway. After I explained what happened, I was allowed to move. Thank God! I don't know what they did to Chaz. I just know that a couple of days later, they told him he was unable to stay in the room. Either he found a new roommate or he would be charged for two living quarters. Chaz and I never talked after the whole ordeal. He was upset because I moved out. He didn't think it was a big deal. But it was, to me. I knew I had to get out the moment he told the girl he would see her again in two weeks. There was no way I was going to go through more sleepless nights and not having the respect I deserved. Chaz was kicked out at the end of the year. He was expelled for earning unacceptable grades……again.

It was sad to see what happened to Chaz. He wasn't a dumb guy. He simply allowed the freedom of college to get the best of him. Unfortunately, Chaz was not the first at Ashland to flunk out. There must have been at least ten like Chaz, both male, female, and Black, that were dismissed from the University because of the same reasons. But why? How could anyone get as far as college and throw their life away? I'd get so angry to see new kids just toss their education right out the window. I realized the freedom in college was the downfall of many minority students who allowed themselves to slack off on work and classes.

College life was an experience where one had to force him/herself to get down to work when it was time. There was time for fun, but college could get the best of you if you allowed it to happen. The students who were dismissed were not strong enough to deal with the temptations of college life. It hurt to see how fast friends came and left. I vowed I would never allow myself to slack off. I couldn't. Being in college was not all just for me. I was there for my family, my close friends, my teachers, my church, my community, my "barrio", Father, and my people. I was unyielding. I was not going to allow anything or anybody to compromise my future. This is what Mrs. Kennard meant when she'd tell her students, "School is not for me it's for you!"

Chapter 14
SOPHOMORE YEAR

After some advice from Father, I decided to take out more money on my school loans to pay for a double room. It was nice. I had my own room, my own things, and my own privacy. It may have been somewhat lonely at times, but it forced me to get out on the yard and get involved with other activities. I must admit that moving out turned out to be the best thing. Although it was costly, it was for the better. I tried the roommate thing and it didn't work. Maybe it was me. Maybe I was the cause of both failures with both of my roommates. Both experiences made me realize that I was not a very easy person to live with. I demand a lot from a person whom I share a roof with like order, respect, cleanliness, and communication. The four characteristics that, in my opinion, were essential in a shared living condition. You have to have these things in order to live with fewer problems and less headaches.

Sophomore year was the most enjoyable year by far as far as acting was concerned. I was cast to play the role of Chief Brown Bear in the musical, <u>Little Mary Sunshine,</u> and Crooks in the play,

Of Mice and Men. The character Crooks was a major challenge since it was a Black character. At the time, I was angry because I felt I wasn't given the chance to prove my acting in a normal role. Up to this point, I had been given the role of a Latino, two rapists, an Indian, and a Black man. I felt bad. I wanted to be acknowledged as an actor of all roles, not just ethnic roles. Although I felt bad, I made the best of it. And, it turned out for the best. Not only did I receive wonderful reviews in the paper for Chief Brown Bear, I also enjoyed wearing the beautiful authentic Native American costume which was the best costume in the show. Chief Brown Bear has been one of my all time favorite roles I've ever done. The year was complete with my initiation into Alpha Psi Omega, the theater honorary fraternity, and my award for outstanding actor of the year in a supporting role. There could not have been a better ending as far as theater was concerned.

When I wasn't at the theater working on a set or rehearsing for a show, I was in the gym watching the women practice volleyball. After days and days of sitting in the bleachers and watching practice, I built up enough nerve to befriend the coach and offer to help. I was ecstatic when she called me to line judge the home matches. It was great because as I earned college work study for working the matches, I was helping out with tuition, and had the opportunity to see how volleyball was played at a college level.

Even though I wasn't playing, I enjoyed being a part of the team through line judging and spectating.

As I watched from the stands, I focused on the playing and coaching style of the team. Boy was it different from CSA. During practice, the coach wasn't as nice as she was off the court. She was tough. She worked those girls during practice like I could not believe. I used to think, "If our coach at CSA ever tried something like that, he'd get laughed right off the court." There was no way my high school team could have gone through the rigorous practice these girls went through. It seemed to me like they ate, slept, and talked volleyball. I was in complete awe!

Although the coach was demanding, the girls respected her and did what she said. It was what it took to be a good team. I remember thinking, "If I ever became a coach, I would want my team to respect me like the women respected their coach." I thought, "Maybe, one day I will get a position in a building, teaching Theater or Spanish and coaching the school's volleyball team." What a fantastic thought! And it wasn't too far-fetched. If I played my cards correctly, there was no reason I couldn't end up with everything in life I wanted, all in one place at the same time. Deep down inside, I knew I could make it happen. I became so enthralled with volleyball, I decided to try and start a men's volleyball team just as I had done at CSA.

I wrote a couple of letters to the college athletic director and to the president asking for their support in my endeavors to start a team. Surprisingly, I was supported and told I should go ahead with the project. After making a few signs and planning an agenda for a small informational meeting, I was astonished to have more than forty guys show up. My continuous determination to start a team was successful. Ashland entered a men's volleyball team in the Midwestern Intercollegiate Volleyball Association my sophomore year. I was not only playing on the team but handled most of the coaching and managing. In our very first year, we accomplished a record of 26-09. The last match was played in the gymnasium in front a big crowd. Men's volleyball became the topic of discussion all around the yard. It even made the town's paper and the school inquirer. Another dream had come true; I was coaching and playing volleyball at a college level. I was on cloud nine.

Jazzy

My efforts could not have happened without Jeff. Jeff lived next door to me. He was a White kid from Pennsylvania. He was a cool and silly guy and always managed to make me laugh about something. He liked rap and hip hop and was awesome on the turn table. Every time we had a party, Jeff was the D.J. That's how he got the name Jazzy Jeff. Jazzy Jeff was the music coordinator for the rapper Fresh Prince. Jazzy liked the name because it made him feel accepted by the brothers and sisters on the yard. He and I were two of the few non-blacks who hung out with the brothers and sisters on the yard.

Jeff played volleyball in high school. I was surprised when he told me that volleyball was interscholastic in Pennsylvania. He was surprised when I explained to him that in Cleveland it wasn't interscholastic, only a student activity. It was because of Jazzy that I learned the intricacies and technical aspects of the sport. When it came to coaching, Jazzy and I made all the decisions together.

Jazzy was a Senior and only needed one more semester to graduate; it was beyond my comprehension why he did what he did. Little did anyone realize he was going through a lot, more than anyone ever gathered. If I had known what he was up to, I would have done my damndest to change his mind.

It all started when Jazzy and a group of students from the college went to North Carolina to help rebuild the city after the destruction by Hurricane Hugo. I don't know what went on down there, but I do know the city left a huge impression on Jazzy. All he talked about spring semester was about going back to get a job at a radio station. Jazzy was a communication/broadcasting major. His dream was to become a disc jockey in a radio station somewhere. He became so infatuated with his dream that he even thought about dropping out in the middle of the semester and going to North Carolina to realize his dream. North Carolina was going through rebuilding. It was to be where he would make his start as a D.J. It didn't help matters that Jazzy was failing his classes. That gave him all the more reason to leave. In mid April of his last semester, senior year, Jazzy packed his things and left. Just like that. His plan was to tell his parents once he arrived in North Carolina. We thought he was crazy. But we supported his decision to leave because we could see it in his eyes that he was determined. He had a passion that everyone believed would drive him to making his dream come true.

Jazzy kept in touch with me and our little group. He'd call once in a while to say he was okay and having a good time. He always managed to dodge the answers to "Where are you living?" or, "Is there a number where you can be reached?" He simply would respond he was staying with a friend. Later, we realized that Jazzy had done all of this for a girl he fell in love with when he went to help rebuild the city. I am assuming she was the whole reason behind Jazzy's wild decision to throw his degree out the window. What love does to a man!

Jazzy became part of our group during the end of the first semester. We called ourselves T.I.P. which stood for "The #1 Posse." T.I.P. was the life of Ashland when it came to sporting events. We'd sit in the stands or bleachers and cheer the entire time. The crowd loved our little posse. Before the basketball and football games, people would come over and ask me where our group would be sitting. Everyone wanted to sit next to us to cheer on the teams. As a matter of fact, on several occasions the head coaches approached us to ask if we could be extra loud for the games against Ashland's arch rivals. We really knew how to get the crowd started. The games were the best times I had at Ashland. Those were the moments when I felt the most school spirit. It was important to me since I was rejected by the cheering squad my freshman year when I asked if I could be a cheerleader. At the time, Ashland was an all female squad, and from what I understood it had always been just a female squad. I guess it was odd, too odd, for a boy to ask to be a male cheerleader. Of course for me it wasn't out of the ordinary since I was a cheerleader at CSA.

    There were only five people in our posse, but by the end of my sophomore year, we had initiated Jazzy and Shep and a couple more. Shep was a freshman when we initiated him. He just started hanging around the posse, and later in the year we initiated him into T#1P.

    Shep was the one who called me to tell me about Jazzy. He called just after the end of the semester. He was at a party in Oberlin when he received the tragic news about Jazzy. Jazzy killed himself in North Carolina!

It was unreal! After getting the full story from his parents, I realized Jazzy had committed suicide because he was deeply depressed. Jazzy's mom sent me the letter they found next to his body. I am still not sure of the exact facts, even though I have read his suicide letter over and over. The letter talked about a girl and her daughter whom apparently Jazzy became very close to. He talked about not having any more meaning to his life and that there wasn't anything else he could do to make his life complete. It sounded like Jazzy and this girl broke up and it left him heartbroken. It might have been that this is who Jazzy was staying with all the while, and after their break up, he had no place to go and no one to turn to. He was probably financially unstable and had no place to stay or go. He knew he couldn't go home, and school was out for the summer. Jazzy probably felt ashamed as he felt his world suddenly come crashing down on him. I knew how he felt. I had been there before. Sometimes, ending the suffering and the agonizing seems like the only logical thing to do. Jazzy mentioned in his letter he simply wanted all the hurt to stop.

I became ill when I read the last page of the letter. He asked his parents to notify his closest friends of his expiration. The list of names was huge; from top to bottom. I lost it when I noticed that the first name on the paper read, "Spanky" my partner in crime."

After getting in contact with the rest of the posse, we decided to have a memorial for him the following fall in the chapel on the yard. It was an intense meeting once we had all gathered. I was surprised to hear and see the different reactions from the group. After embracing each other and crying for a while, we talked about Jazzy's suicide. Some felt sorry that he had suffered alone with no one there to share in his suffering. Others felt like myself, frustrated that we didn't detect his depression while he was on the yard. Some, surprisingly, were angry with Jazzy for taking his life. One member expressed her discontent by saying suicide was the easy way out of his problems and it was selfish because he left us behind to grieve his death. I was thankful for the posse and the group of friends I had. They helped me to get through what was another awful moment in my life. Not only was Jazzy my next door neighbor, teammate, posse brother, and friend, but he was also the closest friend I had made in college.

The memorial we had for him was nice. We had a candlelight walk to the volleyball court in the gym, and later we went to the chapel where I and a few of his friends gave small recollections of Jazzy's accomplishments. We ended the ceremony with a cassette tape Jazzy made after he left the yard. The tape was a music mix he recorded for us. In it he spoke about his adventures in North Carolina as well as his memories of the posse and the good times we had during his stay on the yard. Needless to say, once his voice was heard, the entire place became very emotional. I think it was healthy in a way since it brought his friends together. The gathering was also an opportunity for all of us to say goodbye.

Chapter 15
JEROME

The summer prior to junior year, I was fortunate to have found a job working as a theater instructor for a summer youth program. The job was right up my alley since I was studying to become a theater teacher. The camp's theme was centered around the Arts. The campsite was at the Karamu House in Cleveland. Karamu is a theater center which focuses on the African American Actor. Most of the productions at Karamu are Black based with black actors. The summer job was perfect for me.

I was assigned as the camp theater instructor. My job was to teach stage movement and pantomime to the children. I was given a group of ten kids to teach for the summer. In the group was a nine year old little boy named Jerome. Jerome was the quietest of the entire group. Although he did not say very much, Jerome was kind hearted and very sweet. Jerome took a liking to me and I to him. He never left my side. I liked that Jerome became close to me. It was a good feeling to be wanted and liked. The last day of camp, Jerome embraced me and would not let me go. All he did was hold on to me and cry. He wouldn't say anything; he just cried. It took his mom and a friend to unhook the grasp he had on me. All I could do was hug him back as tears rolled down both our faces. I realized I became an important person in Jerome's life. He was also important to me. I consoled him by promising to come see him even though camp was over.

From here on, Jerome became my little son. As I got to know him and his family, I learned and discovered many things.

Jerome was one of four children. Jerome and his sister Aria have the same father; Danon, his younger brother, and Dalona, the baby sister had different fathers. Jerome's mom was raising all four by herself, and although she had a new boyfriend (whom she was pregnant by at the time), she was struggling financially. I took Jerome under my wing; I picked him up regularly. He came to my house where my family fell in love with him and embraced him as part of the family. That summer, most of the money I made at Karamu went for Jerome's school clothes and summer outfits. I remember how happy it made me to see him carry all the bags of clothes up his front porch steps. I made him promise to take care of them, and he did. He was so proud of his brand new clothes!

My biggest concern was Jerome's mother. I wanted her to understand that what I was doing for Jerome was because I fell in love with him, not because I was trying to show her out or make her feel like I felt sorry for him. Those weren't my intentions. I just wanted Jerome to be happy. For the most part, I think he was. I was relieved after talking to Jerome's mother. She expressed her gratitude and reassured me she was not offended by me gestures to Jerome. I wanted to help. I am grateful I had the opportunity to lend a hand. Besides, when it came to Jerome, I wasn't the only one spoiling him. My family also took part in spoiling him.

The hard part was saying goodbye when it came time to go back to school. At first, it was difficult convincing him I would be back. I think in his mind, he thought I was not coming back at all. I say this because when I dropped him off at home just before going back to Ashland, Jerome became very upset. It was awful! My stomach and throat ached. If I could have taken him to college with me, I would have.

Every time I came home to visit, I'd go see Jerome and take him out or bring him home with me. I wanted him to know I would always be there for him. During the year, I missed him so much I'd leave after my last Friday class and drive home to see him. Sometimes, I'd drive to Cleveland, pick him up and bring him back to Ashland with me for the weekend. It was 75 miles to Cleveland, and 75 miles to Ashland, times four since I'd have to drive him back Sunday afternoon and return for classes Monday morning. There were even trips when I didn't stop in to see my folks. Of course, they never knew I was in town. Had my mom discovered I came to Cleveland and didn't come see her, she would have been hurt. I missed "J-man" so much I took that risk.

Ashland had a "Little Sibling" weekend once a year. Its purpose was to expose young children to college. Jerome loved it! He enjoyed his trips to Ashland. He promised me he would do well in school and one day make it to college. I hoped giving him a taste of college would influence him for the future to come. For three semesters, I continued to bring Jerome to Ashland.

I watched him grow up from that nine year old little boy to a young gentleman. And my God, did he grow up fast. During my two remaining years at Ashland, it seemed as though Jerome had jumped into someone else's body.

Jerome became a member of a singing group just as I had met him. The group was Jerome's median to become a performer, a rap star. To support him, I did what I could by getting him into CSA. At the time CSA, ran from third to twelfth grade. It was tough getting in because of the interest the school had drawn district wide. I went to Mr. Steinmetz for help. I hoped he could pull some strings. I don't know if it was because of Mr. Steinmetz that Jerome got in, all I know is Jerome was accepted to CSA for fifth grade. I was so happy for him! Jerome was bubbling over with excitement. He could hardly wait! As I started my Junior year, Jerome was starting his first year at my Alma Mater. CSA was good for Jerome. It exposed him to all aspects of the arts, and it also gave him the opportunity to work on his dream...music, singing, and rapping.

    Needless to say, I was the proud Godfather. That was the title Jerome gave me. I guess he needed a label for me to explain who I was to his friends since they continued to ask, "Hey Jerome, who is that?" I didn't mind. The title fit perfectly. It was as if God had put Jerome into my life and I in his. "Jerome's Godfather" is how I was referred to from then on.

Chapter 16
JUNIOR YEAR

Spring semester of sophomore year, I added another major to my course load; Spanish. I made the decision after consulting with my theater professor. He was concerned it would be difficult for me to find a teaching position with merely a degree in theater education. He suggested I have a backup plan just in case I could not find a job teaching theater. Since I was a native Spanish speaker, he advised me to look into Spanish as a double major. Actually, it was to be a triple major since I was already majoring in education and theater. I was fortunate to have befriended the head of the foreign language department.

Mrs. Smith offered some helpful insight in regards to the requirements of majoring in Spanish. As it turned out, I was able to test out of some of the Spanish courses and was given credit for them. By the end of the semester, I was majoring in Education, Theater *and* Spanish. I should have had my brain examined! It was extremely difficult juggling three majors since I had to stay active in theater to maintain my scholarship. In addition, I had a responsibility to the volleyball team I'd created, to be operative in the university minority club, the Spanish club, Delta Sigma Pi, the theater Club, Alpha Psi Omega, and keep up with my studies. Let's just say I had an extremely busy junior year. I spent most of my evenings in the library or at my favorite place, the writing lab.

My last semester as a sophomore and my first semester as a junior, I took 20 and 21 credit hours. What in the heck was I thinking? Surprisingly, it was not as overwhelming as I had anticipated. I discovered something interesting about myself. I had become the type of person that needed to have a million things going on in order to function effectively. It sounded crazy! But I enjoyed the pressure and the challenges of being a triple major. I was able to handle the work and still earn good grades.

I didn't do much acting my junior year. My focus was on directing. Directing had always been one of my passions since CSA. Directing was also my big chance to bring Black actors into the department. It wasn't easy convincing my friends to do acting since the reputation of the department wasn't good due to the lack of minority participation. Even so, my friends did not let me down.

My first directing project was a scene from <u>And Miss Reardon Drinks A Little</u>. Three of my closest girlfriends agreed to help me get a grade. They acted out a scene in front of the entire theater department. To my astonishment, the scene received many compliments for fine direction and acting. Those in the department who supported me were so pleased to finally have some new faces involved in the theater. I received several little notes congratulating me for taking a risk and opening the doors to new people. My homegirls were acknowledged for their acting and invited to audition for upcoming performances. I was so proud of my friends. They did a fantastic job!

The final assignment of the semester was to direct a self selected one act play. Coincidentally, this was the same semester the department invited an actor from New York to Ashland to share his poetry work with the University and community. Mr. Keenon Brown visited our directing class the morning after his presentation. He talked about his work and his struggles as an actor in the big city. He inspired me! I could tell by the way he talked that acting meant the world to him. It was then I realized my own passion had died. The passion I once had, the desire I possessed as a high school actor, was gone. I instantly felt so sad. Realizing my loss, I managed to awaken that excitement I once had. Like the summer I spent at Chautauqua my junior year at CSA. Like the fire I felt when I performed in front of my beloved CSA family. Mr. Brown had rekindled my enthusiasm for theater.

During his visit, Mr. Brown talked about a play he had

written. He invited anyone in my directing class to use the play as their final directing project. At first, no one volunteered. I waited for a couple of days to pass before asking if anyone had taken him up on his invitation. Since no one did, I chose to do his play. My professor informed Mr. Brown someone had taken the play. He was so delighted he decided to extend his visit until opening night. What had I gotten myself into? As if I hadn't had enough on my mind!

At our year ending theater banquet, The Cretan Bull won the best one act play of the year! My actors won the awards for best lead and supporting role of the year, and once again I was in the town paper. Persevering had paid off! I was overrun with joy! Using what I learned at CSA and what I was currently learning at Ashland landed The Cretan Bull two consecutive sold out shows!

Doing the play helped me to discover my true passion was directing.

It was the one aspect of theater life where I felt most ardent. I thoroughly enjoyed bringing out the actor in individuals. It made me feel good to see my actors as they transformed characters into real people. Learning how to mold the ability to act in people was great. It was exciting watching actors bring a scene to life. It was magical! Directing became a dream. I wanted to become a director! But how? How would I ever realize such a dream?

To this day, unfortunately, I still have not found the answer. Although directing and teaching come hand in hand, I feel unaccomplished. But I don't want to be misunderstood. There *is* happiness in my work with my students. Nevertheless, it has been difficult to ascertain the complete satisfaction I have been yearning. The worst part is knowing that unless one day I decide to take my chances and just get up and pursue my directing dream, it probably will never happen. It is safe to say that I haven't built up enough courage to "just do it"...yet.

The Spanish department also became a very important part of my life. I was invited to apply for membership into Sigma Delta Pi, the national Spanish honorary. I was initiated at the end of the semester. Becoming proficient in the language was my major goal. I knew how to speak Spanish fluently but had very little knowledge about literature and grammar. I concentrated my efforts on learning every aspect of my language and culture. Mrs. Smith became my closest friend. She encouraged me to go to Spain for a semester. It was a difficult decision as well as a costly and somewhat frightening one. The United States was at war with Iraq, and it was a dangerous time to travel. Mom was hesitant. And after President Bush's press conference discouraging Americans from flying abroad, she was not only against it, she forbade me from making the trip. After realizing all the scholarship money I would lose, and the fact that a trip to Spain was only offered every other year, she reluctantly changed her mind. I was to leave just as "Desert Shield" became "Desert Storm."

Seville, Spain

It was now or never. There was no way I would ever get to go if I passed up the chance. Mom said it was my decision. So, I decided to do it! By the end of the semester, I made all the arrangements. I left for Seville, Spain on January 22, 1991.

Finances were extremely tight. Spending money came from working the volleyball matches and my savings from working winter break at McDonalds. My plane fare, tuition, room and board all came from a student loan. Father was my other saving grace. He donated money for my trip.

Seville was cold. It didn't snow, but boy was it cold! I wasn't prepared for what I experienced. The home where I was placed along with ten other Americans was not at all what I had anticipated. From the beginning, I knew it was going to be a rough and challenging semester. The house, like most all homes in Seville, did not have central heating and very little water pressure. I shared a room with a guy named David who, thank God, was very friendly. He was the only good thing about the home until things got so bad he was forced to find another host family. Like me, David couldn't handle the horrible conditions of the home. After a week, he asked to be moved to another home. We were down to nine students.

The woman of the house, Mabel, ran it like a student hostel. The atmosphere in the home was cold-hearted and very impersonal. I was sad I had not been given a real home. Coming from a Latino background, I was surprised at the lack of warmth and friendliness in the home. When I first arrived, I anticipated a kinder greeting with open arms and more excitement as I was told would happen. I'll never forget how disappointed I was when Mabel opened the door. She asked me how many bags I had and pointed me up the stairs to my room. The only thing she said was, "Jore late. Deener weel be ten minutes."

I was in complete shock. I didn't know what to do. My first instincts were to turn around and go back to the airport. I felt so alone for that instant when we met. The emotions of being away from my home, and my family, suddenly flooded my heart. A hard painful sore engulfed my stomach. It was as though I swallowed something that wasn't good for me. I had just finished a thirteen hour journey, and was still dealing with the machine guns the airport guards welcomed us with when we arrived in Seville. It hit me then that my trip to Europe was a risky one. Had I put my life in danger by traveling? Dealing with the doubt and being frightened about being and feeling so alone was enough to make a person crazy. The greeting at the door made me feel like total crap. This was not what I had dreamed my much anticipated trip would be like.

Not only was the home atmosphere frigid but, boy, so were the nights. I was instantly reminded of the thermostat on the wall in my mom's living room. What a commodity it was at home to simply get up and turn up the heat. It was during the long freezing nights I sat in bed realizing the simple pleasures of life. For Sevillians, things like thermostats and hot water tanks were things only rich people possessed. These were the little things that went unnoticed in my house. What a discovery it was for me to realize how I took things for granted.

I might have known something was odd when Mabel suggested we save our two liter bottles of pop. The only way to stay warm and get to sleep was snuggling next to a warm two liter bottle of hot water. The ten of us were given one blanket, one very thin blanket, and a roll of toilet paper for a two week period. When David left the home, yes, I was sad. But at the same time, I was kind of happy since I thought I could get his blanket and his roll of toilet paper. To my dismay, someone had thought about it first. When I began looking through his empty cupboards for the blanket and paper, they were gone. Someone had beaten me to it.

Things just got worse and worse after David left. The food

became a serious issue. Mabel's meals were unpleasant! They consisted of bologna sandwiches and fish soup. The soup was served for lunch and sometimes the same fish soup for dinner. The stench that came from over cooking and reheating fish was the part I detested the most. Everyone knew the food was spoiled when the aroma of rotten fish permeated the air during supper. At one point, I realized the only way to eat would have to be preparing food myself or eating out. Unfortunately, I learned quickly cooking in the home was not going to be an option. We were told, after one of the Americans made some hot chocolate, that the kitchen was off limits. Being in or using the kitchen was out of the question. Since our presence in the kitchen was forbidden, making personal meals was unheard of. We were told to stay away from the kitchen until called for meals. I realized it was the Spanish way when it came to kitchens, men, cooking, washing dishes, and setting the table. Men were just not supposed to do those things. It really wasn't as much of a problem for me since I was used to the "No men allowed in the kitchen" rule. I was reminded of my own home where my father and I were waited on by Mom and my sisters. (Although as the years progressed, I was told more and more to, "Get up and get it yourself." I guess this is what it meant to be "Americanized." So much for keeping with customs and Latino beliefs.)

My favorite (and cheapest) fast food was the Spanish

appetizers called "Tapas." One could find tapas anywhere. They were in mostly all the pubs and taverns. Although tapas became a substitute for Mabel's horrible meals, it was a detriment to my pocket. I was going broke fast. As if keeping warm and being hungry weren't bad enough, taking showers or simply cleaning up was horrendous! The worst part of Mabel's house, hostel, or whatever you want to call it, was the water, or the lack of water. There was no water pressure, and it was ice cold! It was then I discovered water tanks did not exist in most homes. Those families who had hot water owned electrical shower heads. During January, February, and halfway through March, cleaning up consisted of towel baths and washing up with ice cold water. I was not a happy camper, to say the least. I had to do something! But what?

The first two months of my semester were absolutely dreadful.

I think the most detrimental part of the ten of us under the same roof was the fact we were not practicing the language. How could anyone practice a foreign language living with ten Americans? I became so depressed and so homesick, I just wanted to pack up and leave. I managed to refocus my life after deciding to take a trip into Portugal.

Fatima

One day, I got up and, without debating, bought an eighteen-dollar round trip bus ticket from Seville to Lisbon, Portugal. My destination was the shrine of Our Lady Of Fatima. I hungered for rejuvenation. I needed to find something that would help me refocus and get over being homesick. It didn't help matters that there was a war going on and it seemed like my decision to go to Spain was not serving its purpose at all. I thought this would be a beautiful gesture of faith. What a wonderful way to get back on track.

I don't remember exactly how I heard about Fatima. I simply remember someone telling me it was not very far from Seville. I had to go not only for myself but for my mom and my father. I had to visit our Blessed Mother and personally thank her for all her intercessions up to that point in my life.

My father's life after the automobile accident, Adriana's life from almost choking to death, and most importantly, getting me to where I was in life... one year closer to graduating from college, were just a few of things for which I wanted to say "Thank You." My devotion to the Blessed Mother became stronger after my visit to Fatima. Words cannot express how it felt to be on the same grounds where she appeared to Jacinta, Francisco, and Lucia. I was overpowered with peace and content during my visit to the Lady.

Turning to God had always been my way of redirecting my thoughts, aims, goals and precepts. Since the tragedy of my attack, the loneliness of losing my close friends, and all the other challenges in my life, it became second nature to look to Christ for guidance and recharging of faith in times of depression, and uncertainness. I realized how grateful I was to have the ability to seek God and the Blessed Mother in challenging times. I was grateful for having a mom that taught me how to pray and find peace of mind in prayer. How fortunate I was for having Mom and Father D. I just kept thinking how truly blessed I was to be in Fatima. I felt a sense of sadness as I wished someone like Mom or Father D. could have been there to share those joyous moments with me. How could I ever express to them or anyone for that matter, how important in my life was this trip?

I took the chance to see other parts of Lisbon during my trip to Fatima. It was a magnificent experience, and although I did not share the experience to the Basilica with anyone, writing about it is my opportunity to reveal the impact of the Blessed Mother in my life and to convey how beautiful my trip was to Fatima.

What a treat Seville was in the Spring. The highlight of the semester was "Semana Santa" (Holy Week), "Feria" (Fair) and Carmen. Semana Santa and Feria were two of the most spectacular and most breathtaking events I have ever seen and witnessed in all my life. The processions of the statues of Christ and the Blessed Mother through the streets of Seville were unlike anything I have ever seen or imagined. No one at home would ever believe an entire city shut down for a whole week to proclaim their eight hundred year tradition. The preparation for such an event was shocking as Seville worked together to realize this grand event. It was proof that any society could do whatever they set their minds to do. Seville was a town possessed with pride in their display of Holy Week.

Feria was the second phenomenon of the semester. Two weeks after Easter and Holy Week, the Sevillians once again, and with the same furor, upheld another yearly spectacle. A sand lot was converted into a city of lights where a week of festivities would take place. Feria, or Fair, was Seville's other magnificent spring event. The people displayed their attire dressed in typical Flamenco dress during the day as they rode beautifully decorated horses.

As the night appeared, the horses disappeared, and the "casetas" or cabins became filled with people, wine, and the dancing of Sevillanas, the typical folk dance of the region. This spectacular event was truly a celebration of new life. Sevilla's fine commitment to tradition was evident as the people of Seville put on another unbelievable event.

Although my experience in Mabel's home was not as I hoped it would be, I did find some fortune. I met a wonderful girl named Carmen.

Carmen was an American girl who was also studying in Seville. She was in a different program and had come to Seville to study for a year. Carmen was sitting in Mabel's living room helping her son with English homework when I met her. I immediately fell in love with her.

When our eyes meet, it filled my whole world with warmth.

Suddenly, every preoccupation I had in Spain was gone. Just like that, I felt no worries, sorrows, pain, or loneliness. I stood in the middle of the room waiting for Mabel's son to introduce me. When he didn't, I apologized for interrupting and introduced myself. I made small talk with Carmen, asking her where she was from and where she was living. I suggested without thinking if she would have a Coke with me after she was done tutoring. When she agreed, I felt my eyes wide open, my heart was in my throat, and as if though my palms became instant water faucets. I became the happiest and most excited person in the world. It was the most absolutely crazy thought, but I knew I was in instant love.

Carmen didn't look like an ordinary American student. She didn't have that "Yankee" look. She had her own look, her own way, her own aura. As we got to know each other, I discovered she was Portuguese and French. Her eyes were light green, her hair was long and light brown, and her body was out of this world. The one aspect that made her special was her gorgeous smile. Every time Carmen smiled at me, my insides turned to mush.

After the initial meeting, we saw each other every day. She and I became friends. At first, we were pals. That is what I loved the most about our relationship. I fell in love with our friendship first, and fell in love with her second. I felt Carmen was falling in love with me too. Although she never said it, I felt it.

After class one day, we went to the plaza to talk. I enjoyed talking with Carmen. Having someone to talk with was great. I could listen to her talk to me for hours. At the plaza, Carmen expressed she didn't want to fall in love to have her heart be broken later on. I imagined Carmen was referring to the end of the semester. School would be over, and we would go our separate ways. Falling in love, to her, was a mistake. A broken heart was not something she wanted to experience. I wasn't concerned with the future. I desired only to live the "here and now." It wasn't until later that I became numb realizing that in a couple of months I would have to say goodbye to the girl of my dreams.

Since the thought depressed me, I made every effort not to think about the end of the semester. I just wanted to enjoy her company and live each moment I had with her to the fullest. We both agreed to forget about the inevitable and enjoy the present. And although we never discussed the end of the semester again, I could feel the depression lingering in the depths of our minds.

Carmen studied dance in the states. She majored in dance in college since dancing was what she had been doing all her life. Her father owned a dance studio in France and wanted Carmen to come work and live with him. Carmen felt stuck in the middle of her parent's divorce. She liked the idea about France but was reluctant because she didn't want to leave her mom in the states. For me, it could not have been a more perfect relationship. She was into dance, I was into theater. It was match made in heaven. While it seemed to be a one in a million match, it was the most frustrating feeling. All I could think was why couldn't we have met in the states? Why? I was mortified at the thought of losing my could-have-been, soul mate.

Our last night together, Carmen informed me she had decided to take her dad's offer in France. She was to be the newest staff member as a ballet instructor in his dance school. Her dad needed her right away since the new season was approaching. It meant she would not be finishing the semester in Seville. Our last night, although melancholic, was unforgettable.

We walked the banks of the Seville's river, "El Guadarquibil," as we watched the stars disappear and the sun rise. During the early morning, we stopped on the foot of the bank to rest. There, under a big tree, we fell asleep in each other's arms. I had never felt so comfortable with anyone since Scotland and Norma.

It was the same feeling but different. With Norma it was more of a physical first time tie. With Carmen, it was sweet, romantic, warm, genial. As the stars faded into the daylight, I remember making a wish for time to freeze forever. Feeling like this was the way I hoped to feel with the person with whom I would spend the rest of my life. Although I was content, I couldn't help but to be disenchanted. Again, my only thought was, "Why couldn't I have met my Carmen in the states?"

My time with Carmen was one of those things I have come to accept as being a small scene in my life's play. A play with many scenes before the finality. If it was truly meant to be, I believed one day, Carmen and I would cross paths again. After I said goodbye to Carmen, I decided to move out of Mabel's Hostel since it was the hostility that was making me even more miserable. I was fortunate in that I was given the latitude to select another living condition just before Holy week and Feria. I moved into a more "family-like" home...so I thought.

The program director informed me there was a home available in the downtown area of Seville.

It was a good home with an older couple and two daughters, Mariana and Rosalin, who were in college. My two new host sisters were wonderful *in the beginning*. They took me all over Seville and showed me a great time. At first, I loved the change. The family seemed more in tune with family life and customs. They treated me as though I was a family member. This was a big change from Mabel's Hostel. At least now I felt as if I was in a real family. We ate meals together, watched television, and most importantly, spoke Spanish. English was not permitted, especially during supper. Although I knew how to speak Spanish, I needed lots of work. I discovered what I had been speaking all my life was broken Spanish. This was my opportunity to speak a better quality Spanish. I was thrilled!

The sisters introduced me to their circle of friends. It was nice meeting new people my age. I learned so much about Spanish young adult life. I was excited about all the new friends I made. I enjoyed spending time with them and practicing the language. I realized through my relationships with my new friends that this Spanish was very different from the Spanish I grew up with. I found it interesting how different my Colombian upbringing was from that of the Spanish people.

A week or so after the sisters and I continued to venture into Seville, their friends began visiting me daily. It didn't seem like a big deal at first.

It never crossed my mind for a moment the visits were becoming a problem with the sisters, particularly the older of the two, Mariana. I realized the more they came to see me, the sisters became angry, jealous, and cold towards me. It was about the fourth visit when I remember seeing it written all over Maraina's face. Antonio, who I was introduced to by Rosalin, came to the door on his brand new motorcycle and asked if I was home. Mariana greeted him and asked him what his plans were for the evening. When he said he came by to take me on a motorcycle ride, her face sank. I remember the wrinkles in her forehead as she tried desperately to keep her facial expressions from giving away her resentment. It wasn't until weeks later that Antonio informed me Mariana had been asking him for a ride on his new BMW motorcycle. He always managed to change the subject since he felt Mariana had a crush on him. Antonio didn't want to lead her on since his feelings for Mariana were not reciprocal.

Antonio was a barber. He came from an established family and a history of barbers. His grandfather, father, and brother owned one of Seville's most prestigious shops. I chuckled when he told me he was a barber. I remembered Alfalfa from the Little Rascals, singing "I'm the Barber Of Seville." Antonio and I became like two brothers. Not a day went by that Antonio did not come over to take me out for a ride on his motorcycle. Antonio was a Godsend. Especially since Carmen had gone to France.

He introduced me to his family and his circle of friends. After classes at the University of Seville, I'd rush home and get ready since I knew Antonio would come to pick me up. I believe it was because of Antonio and his family that I could forget about all the things which were making me sad. I remember looking for the small statue of Our Lady of Fatima in my bag of souvenirs. I wanted to thank her for yet another miracle. When I was at Fatima, I prayed for someone nice to come into my life to help me get through the remaining months of my semester in Seville.

As it turned out, the sisters completely stopped talking to me. I was convinced they'd taken exception to my relationship with Antonio. I overheard Mariana telling her mother Antonio invited me to his beach house on the coast. She was fit to be tied because Antonio did not invite her or Rosalin. Apparently, the sisters had also been anxiously waiting for Antonio to invite them to the beach property, but he never did. When I was invited for the weekend, the sisters fumed.

My new home turned into a nightmare. It made Mabel's hostel look like a royal palace. Things became so bad, the last two weeks before I returned to the states, I asked Antonio if I could stay with him and his family. Because Antonio and I had become so close, I became a part of his family. Thank God they opened their home to me. I was the adopted American son. They became my surrogate family; wonderful, warm and very loving. I will always cherish the treatment I received from them. On my twenty-first birthday, they threw me a surprise birthday party. It made the war, Mabel's hostel, the sisters, Carmen, and being homesick easier to forget.

The trip to Spain could not have ended without an unfortunate incident. My adventure was marred with the awful accident Antonio and I had on our way to the coast one day. He misjudged a curve on our way out of a small village and we wrecked! Luckily I had a protective body suit and helmet. The only thing I had forgotten that day were gloves. The accident completely ruined my right hand, pinkie knuckle, ring finger, and left me with two deep gashes on both palms. A family driving by the wreck saw we were in need of medical attention and offered to take me in their van. They took us to the nearest clinic where a woman scraped the dirt from my open wounds and gave me a shot. The pain I endured was horrendous. All of my challenges of the semester swarmed into a final moment of agony. I think after getting over the initial shock of the accident, I felt there was nothing more that could happen to me, besides losing my life. The evil on was busy; busy, busy, busy!

Antonio was so apologetic and nervous. He must have said, "Lo siento mucho, Guillermo," ("I am so sorry William") a thousand times. I remember feeling more bad for him and his motorcycle than for my wounded hands. Initially, we were going to attempt riding back to Seville on the bike, but I was shaking with fear too much. My hands were wrapped with bandages and it was difficult, as well as painful, to hold on.

Antonio found a bus station in the small town. He purchased a ticket for me to get back to Seville. I discovered later, Antonio drove his bike all the way back to Seville despite the condition it was left in after the accident. He visited me later that evening.

When I arrived at home with all my injuries, there was no answer at the door. I sat on the steps waiting for someone to come. About an hour went by when the doors opened. It startled me since I thought there was no one home. Mariana attempted to explain she didn't answer the door because she thought I was a beggar. In all my life, I'd never felt so provoked. It took every ounce of my being to keep from completely going off. I was so agitated I could feel the blood pulsating in my wounded hands. I let Mariana have it! I verbally went off on her when I noticed her smirking at my injuries. After I was done yelling I managed to calm down enough to go into my room. I fell on my knees to ask God and the Blessed Mother for patience, strength, fortitude, and the will to finish out the semester without any more negative incidents.

Moments later, I heard a knock on the door. As I peered out of my balcony window onto the street, I saw Antonio's wrecked bike. I overheard Mariana and Antonio talking. After listening to her story, I heard him ask if she took the time to look out of the balcony to see who was knocking. She responded she didn't get up because she had been studying for a test.

Antonio defended me, telling her she should have gotten up and answered the door. He ended his conversation abruptly and came upstairs to my room. When he saw me dejected and broken, he didn't ask any questions. I gave in and revealed to Antonio the hostility I had been dealing with since we met. He told me he knew something was going on and believed Mariana knew I was at the door. She probably knew it was me, and to make me angry she decided not to get up and open the door.

Antonio was upset for not informing him of what was going on with Mariana and Rosalin. He felt it was his fault. He felt guilty for the trouble he had caused between me and the sisters. It was then Antonio said he would talk with his parents about me staying the remainder of the time at his home. After Antonio admonished Mariana, I had a gut feeling things would now be worse than ever with the sisters. I felt relieved when he informed me he didn't think it would be a problem. He received permission from his parents and came to get me the next morning.

My incredible semester in Seville concluded with trips to Morocco (Africa), Italica, Badajoz, Granada, and Cordoba. I ended my outings taking an unforgettable fifteen-hour train trip to

Barcelona. My trip to Barcelona was especially unique because the purpose of the trip was to locate my mom's eldest sister, who was a nun for the Little Sister's of The Poor. She lived in a convent just outside Barcelona in a small pueblo called Gava.

What a glorious time I had meeting a real life family member of Mom's family. The visit with my aunt was very dear. I had been her only visitor since she was first sent to Spain back in 1952. It was a precious visit, one that I will never forget! She and the other nuns took me to Montserrat and into the city of Barcelona, which at the time was gearing up for the 1992 Olympics. Meeting her was a revelation. Could my love for the Blessed Mother and my relationship with God be something I inherited from my eldest aunt? I believe my visit with her made it perfectly clear that things do "run in the family."

My experiences in Spain, the people I met, and the places I visited proved to be a big lesson in my life. If I hadn't learned anything, I learned to cherish the little things I had in life. I vowed never to complain about not having certain things. I promised God I would never look a gift towards the mouth. It was engraved in stone and embedded in my head that although I wasn't rich, nor was my family rich, the little things I possessed in the states were a priceless treasure! The insignificant things like running water, central heating, toilet paper (which I never thought as being a luxury), down to the smallest things like having the freedom to roam freely in Mom's kitchen, were things I would never take for granted ever again. It took my experiences in Spain to make me realize how truly blessed I was. And as for the hardships, once again I was convinced when doors close, sometimes slam shut, with faith as a foundation, God always manages to let a crack sneak open.

Life wasn't so critical any more. Little things that bothered me didn't bother me as much. I learned to deal with disappointments dished out by life. I learned to be more relaxed and less stressful. Most importantly, I learned to deal with people and challenges aimed at ruining a good day, a pleasant moment, a nice time, a special event, a learning semester, a fruitful year, a positive week, or a productive month. My approach to obstacles and hindrances radically changed. I had a whole new outlook about life. I learned to be at peace with myself first, with others second. I learned that no matter what, I was the captain of my ship. I discovered it was I who had the control. It was I who had the power over me and all the world that surrounded me. I learned to be self empowered! What a fascinating phenomenon! Too abstract to teach, too aesthetic to describe, too difficult to explain, and too arduous to demonstrate. What a blessed realization!

Junior year was over, and so was the war. The experiences of

Spain would always be inscribed in my mind and heart; I have never told anyone about the downs of my trip to Seville. Upon my return, I wanted everyone to think my semester abroad was fabulous. I wanted to make it seem like nothing went wrong. I convinced all of my family and friends that my trip to Europe was a delightful one. My trip to Spain allowed me to reflect and to grow from both the favorable and unfavorable circumstances and experiences while realizing and discovering my role in life as a human being and as a child of God.

Chapter 17
RETURNING HOME

I felt out of place for a long time after my trip to Spain. Home, the house, the street, the atmosphere, Cleveland, just everything was odd to me. In a way, I felt as if I had lost something. It's difficult explaining exactly what I felt or how I felt. I was having trouble feeling as though I belonged. It took about a week or so until that weird feeling of not belonging went away.

Upon my return, I detected there was something definitely wrong with Mom and my father. Usually when things were quiet, there was something going on. Something bad! At first, I wanted to ask Mom, but I hesitated. Somehow I knew it wasn't going to be pleasant. I was convinced it had to do with finances. Why did I have a strange feeling my parents were eagerly awaiting my return? It wasn't until days later I discovered the house was in foreclosure due to the lack of mortgage payments. When I found out the bank was going to take the house away from my parents, I crumbled. They had been waiting on me to save the house from being lost. It was my father who implied I had money. He made several references to my credit card and the purchases I made in Seville. He suggested I help out with the problem since he had just sent me to Spain. How dare he, I thought? Spain was paid through a school loan. Spending money came from work study, my savings, McDonald's, Father D, Mr. Steinmetz, and the sacrificing contributions Mom made like the three twenty dollar bills she wrapped in a shirt in a care package she sent to Seville for me. Financial help from my father was non-existing. And although I never expected my parents to pay for Spain, I never anticipated they would attempt to take credit for the entire semester's expenditures. Without hesitation and with unbelievable fury, I immediately went to the bank and withdrew my entire credit line on my visa. The house payments were three months overdue. With the attorney fees, the total debt was $850.00. That debt remained on my credit card for the next two and a half years until I began teaching. With the horrible interest rates, the final bill was nearly $2000.00.

    I was so bitter with my parents. I cringed at the thought of knowing I was always going to be the one to save the day. I was furious with them for putting me in that predicament. What would have happened to the family had I not had a credit card? Where would we have ended up? I couldn't figure out what the hell was going on. Why were the house payments so far behind? Where was the money going? I knew where the money wasn't going.

I discovered the reason for the lack of attention to the mortgage payments. It involved a used station wagon Mom and my father had financed while I was in Spain.

It was unimaginable to me how they could get themselves into more debt. I should have (with the risk of getting my teeth knocked out by my father) questioned my parent's decisions concerning the finances in the home. It was obvious to me after the incident with the house payments that my parents had an enormous lack of knowledge when it came to their financial status and their responsibilities involving payments on loans. There was no way we could afford a car with my father working odds and ends and Mom's part time job. When the car dealer people came with a tow truck to repossess the station wagon, it took every bit of energy I had to keep myself from saying, "I told you so," to my parents. My father also stopped paying the loan on the station wagon because it began giving him problems. Soon after they brought the car home, it needed breaks, and a lot of work. My father attempted to take the car back, but they wouldn't pay him any attention. I discovered later my father bought the station wagon under an "as is" policy. The dealership would not take responsibility for the repairs the wagon needed. The wagon was a lemon.

Work wasn't easy to come by since I had arrived late in the

summer from Spain. I could not find a job which would hire me for such a short time. I tried to go back to McDonald's, but they had enough workers. I survived, once again, with the help of Father D.

I worked at the church cleaning the floors and doing other small jobs. I am grateful for the work at the church. It taught me what real work was all about. Working for Father D. was very hard. He demanded excellence and wanted things to be done the correct way. Although at the time it made me upset, I learned how to be a good worker. Working hard built character. Years later, I realized the labor I experienced at the church helped me to work hard in life, never looking for the easy way out or cutting corners

I remember being anxious for the summer to end. I was ready to go back to school and be a senior. Being angry about the car also made me anxious to return to school. Being angry and always in a bad mood made me crazy. The debt on my credit card and the fact that no one cared about my visa bills made me more than ready to move back to school. I was so thoroughly disgusted with everyone. I wanted no part of my family. Although it hurt, it was the way I felt. The burning in my stomach returned when I realized all my future work study money my senior year would be going to the credit card company. How frustrated it made me to think about how hard it was not using the visa in Spain. Thinking about it made me the most emotional. The whole time I was in Spain, I worried about running up my credit card. It was difficult not to charge things I desired. It was even harder not being able to go places with my friends for fear of the credit card bills I would later be faced with. I had managed to keep my credit card within a hundred dollar debt during my semester in Seville.

You can imagine how terrible it was for me to come home after all the sacrifices I made, and be forced to charge almost a thousand dollars on my account. How could they have done that to me, I thought? I was so livid, I could not let the matter go. This whole ordeal later came up again in a huge argument and was the sole reason why I, in great anger, moved out of my parent's home.

Chapter 18
CAREN

I was reintroduced to Caren at the yearly church festival the month after I returned from Spain. I met Caren back in the twelfth grade. Her mother worked with my father at a restaurant where my father washed dishes. Caren was sixteen when I first met her. She was short, had long black hair, cream colored skin, and was very attractive. For me, the best part about Caren was that she was also Colombian.

Caren didn't know a bit of English when I met her. I marveled talking to her because she sounded like my father and Mom. I realized Colombian's have a different dialect from the Puerto Rican dialect which I was use to hearing. She sounded so pure, and so formal. Her words were clear and crisp, unlike the fast, choppy sounds I was used to hearing. It was both different and nice to hear someone from my parent's country other than my parents. Caren and I began seeing each other more and more. I wasn't looking for a girlfriend. Caren coming into my life again was unplanned.

I was so disillusioned with the idea of girlfriends to the point where I thought I would have to be crazy to get involved with someone who was visiting Cleveland from Colombia. I promised myself not to get drawn into anymore girls who were not from Cleveland or for that matter from the states. The cost of doing so could mean more damage to an already broken heart.

I promised myself there would be no way I would get involved with Caren! I was not going to put myself through another disappointment. I left Caren alone. It wasn't until the summer before senior year that we saw each other again after almost four years. She came back to Cleveland to live. I noticed her English had improved a great deal. She wasn't talking to me in Spanish. I guess she wanted me to know she had been practicing since we last saw each other. Caren knew just how far to flirt with me. She'd pull her hair behind her ears exposing her neck and shoulders. I could feel she was interested in me. When we began talking at the festival, I could feel my heart beating faster and faster. Caren hypnotized me with her gaze.

It was odd talking with Caren after four years. Although I had not thought about her since my senior year at CSA, I felt weird inside, like with Norma and Carmen. Courting Caren was very different from Carmen. Because Caren was from Colombia, it intrigued me even more to conquer her love. She expected to be treated very differently from girls I had been with in the past. With

Caren, it was more of a Colombian courting. She believed in traditional chivalry like flowers, candy, holding hands, and pulling out chairs or opening doors. I played along since for me, it was a new experience and an interesting one. Being Colombian did not mean I knew how to court Colombian girls. This was a cool way to see how to date Colombian style.

I learned many things while pursuing Caren. I enjoyed working so hard to win her over. And though I was happy being Caren's boyfriend, I was scared to tell her our time together was to be cut short. She was a very emotional girl. I didn't know how she would take the news that I would be leaving for college. I was going back to Ashland to begin my senior year. Caren was the type of girl who could make an issue of my going away. At one point, she suggested we could stay together if I were to transfer to Cleveland State. Since I knew where she was going with the conversation, I desperately changed the subject. Caren got the picture when she realized I was set to go back no matter what. Now it was a matter of dealing with my leaving. Would a long distance relationship with Caren work?

Caren visited me almost every weekend after I left. At first, our relationship seemed the same. Actually, it was great being apart for a whole week. It made seeing her on the weekend that much more exciting. When she couldn't make it down to Ashland, I drove to

Cleveland to see her. I had to really be careful. I used to sneak to see J-man, so I knew how to go about creeping into Cleveland to see Caren. I didn't like going to Caren's house for fear her mom would tell my father. Since they worked together, I thought Caren's mother would inform my father of my trips to Cleveland. My mom would discover I was visiting Caren and did not stop at home to say hello. It would hurt her feelings and maybe make her upset. So, I always made sure to set up a rendezvous location with Caren.

My relationship with Caren was jaded. I hadn't totally forgotten about Carmen. Deep down inside, she was still fresh in my heart. I don't think I was completely over her. I began to wonder if my being with Caren was a huge mistake. Was I using Caren to block out my saddened heart? Was this a case of being with someone on "the rebound"? Was Caren simply someone to fill the space of "girlfriend" in my life? I was confused. I didn't know how to feel. I became afraid when I saw how much Caren cared for me. When I realized she was falling in love with me, I became apprehensive to continue our relationship. The last thing I wanted to do was hurt Caren. She'd call every day, sometimes five times a day. She wanted to be together every moment possible even if it was over the phone. I realized this balloon of sorts was getting bigger and bigger and I would have to do something before it exploded in my face. By the time I could express how I felt and explain why I felt the way I did, it had been too late. Caren confessed she was in love with me.

I felt horrible because I did not want to cause Caren pain and heartache. She was the best girlfriend anyone could have. She took care of me, was understanding, sweet, loving, and very romantic. She showed her sweet affection with gifts like cologne, cards, stuffed animals and even flowers. I tried to convince myself she was the right girl for me. Maybe I was mixed up and all I needed was to give it a chance. So I did. But it just didn't happen. It didn't click as with Carmen and Norma.

It just didn't click the way I had wished it would. I had become so hurt and felt such disenchantment with relationships that I had built a wall around me. A wall that not even Caren could get through. She constantly expressed how difficult it was to get through to me. It was frustrating for her not to be able to get inside my heart. I just couldn't; the fear of having it be torn out again was too great. I felt vulnerable opening up again. I didn't want to. I was reluctant. I was afraid. The more Caren attempted, the further I pushed her away.

The only time I was able to be open and willing to let my emotions show was with my little son, J-man. Caren reminded me several times how she wished she could be in my world like I allowed J-man in my life. On several occasions, she expressed she actually felt a little jealous that J-man received more attention and affection than she did. There was a lot of truth in that. Jerome was someone I could trust to be honest. He was my little son. His affection and feelings for me were genuine and sincere. He simply wanted me for me, no strings attached, and I felt the same way. Just knowing that my presence in his little life was important to him made me feel so content. Caren wanted the same, but it was not happening.

During my courtship of Caren, she revealed her dreams to me. She wanted to remain in the U.S. and start her own family. She aspired to get married and raise her children the Latino way; instilling culture, customs and traditions in the lives of her children.

She also divulged how she was waiting for the right man to make love to for the first time. I'm convinced the feelings she developed for me was due in part because she felt she had found that "right man" in me.

All my life, I heard about the nightmares men had to endure with girls who hadn't had their first intimate experience. My friends used to scare me with stories of the dangers in dating virgins. Virgins could turn into "fatal attractions." Virgins were said to hold onto their first, no matter what it took, sometimes acting crazy and doing outrageous things. Curtis from Willson once told me he tried to break up with a girl who lost her virginity to him. She went ballistic on him when she caught Curtis with Mercedes. She ranted, raved, and even scratched Curtis' face. He'd say, "Virgins are not to be messed with unless you are serious about the relationship and plan to be together for a long time. A real long time!"

For Caren, being a virgin had tremendous impact on her emotions for me. Unfortunately, I allowed my flesh and desires to think for me in the midst of the moment. Caren lost her virginity to me two months after the start of senior year. There was no turning back! Caren's desire to be by my side became insatiable. She began driving down to Ashland almost five days a week. It was getting out of hand and affecting my school work.

Because of my trip to Spain, I had to get a roommate. It was extremely expensive to keep a single room. When I returned to Ashland, I asked to have a roommate. The thought of not having my own room scared me a bit. I remembered how it was with Jeff and Chaz. I feared having a roommate could land me with the same bad luck I had in the past.

My new roommate was a freshman football player. I called him Flea, short for his last name. Flea was a brother from a small town in Ohio. He came to Ashland on a football scholarship. He was an athlete in every form of the word. He was very fit and very muscular. Flea's athleticism was good for me, since it was because of him I began to lift weights and get into shape. Caren loved it. She benefited from my "being in shape" and made sure to express how she liked to see her man in shorts and t-shirts. Training made me feel good about myself. It also made me feel good to make Caren feel good.

Caren managed to get a hold of Flea and arrange his not being in the room during one of her weekend visits. Although it seemed like a typical evening with flowers, candles, music and her perfume, I was nervous. Somehow, I knew it was to be the night she and I would make love for the first time. At first, I felt unsure about going all the way with Caren. I knew how sacred this was for her. Because Caren was going to allow such an intimate and special thing to occur, she must have really had her mind and heart into our relationship.

I felt guilty inside since I didn't feel as strong as she. This was what she wanted, as I continued to ask her throughout the evening, "Are you sure?" to which she responded, "Yes, because I love you....yes."

Caren thought of everything, from the gorgeous negligee which perfectly adorned her body, down to the long, colored feathers, and rubbing lotions she brought to massage me. As the night progressed, she demonstrated her thoroughness by the small box of contraceptives she had carefully hidden in her bag.

As we kissed I noticed she was trembling. Again, I asked her if this is what she wanted. With a small kiss in my right palm, she nodded yes. She moved my hands slowly. I felt Caren was teaching me what made her feel good, and what she desired me to do. Caren was awesome at making me feel like I was making love to her, as opposed to having sex with her. I learned with our intimacy the difference between the two.

During our adventure and discovery of one another, I was shocked to realize my body was not responding. The entire time we explored each other, I began to feel fear crawling through my body. Could it have been the guilt of not loving Caren the same way she loved me? Or could it have been the thoughts I had about being Caren's first love? I was unsure about the night. Caren being a virgin clouded my mind.

Curtis's words continued to cloud my thoughts. The guys on the yard teased me about Caren. They'd tell me having sex with a virgin was asking for trouble. Caren noticed my fading away and asked was there something wrong. I explained to her I didn't want her to think I was rushing our intimacy. She comforted my concerns by placing her index finger over my lips saying, "Shhhhh."

It didn't take long for my body to awaken after Caren let her negligee straps slide down the sides of her arms, exposing her beautifully curved body. I felt my heart pulsating, and my hands began to sweat. We kissed and caressed. Soon after, Caren suddenly reached under her pillow and pulled out a gold square. It was a sign that she'd had enough exploration. As she tore off the corner and exposed the condom, her eyes closed and her breathing increased. It was clear Caren was nervous as her hands shook a bit.

She clasped on to me and whispered in my ear those three unforgettable words..."I love you." I responded with a smile.

I wondered if making love for Caren was the same as it was for me. I remembered how it felt with Norma. Making love for the first time was like getting on a roller coaster. Climbing up the first giant hill waiting for that inevitable drop while your heart beats with excitement. The adrenalin surges through every inch of your body as it aches and begs for more and more exhilaration. I took my time, assuring Caren our episode would be loving, not sexual.

Before the night was over, we made love several more times. That morning, one golden square remained in the small box.

Caren was wonderful. Making love to her was the most sensuous experiences I've ever had. Our sexual relationship became great. Unfortunately, it became the sole purpose of our being together. The person to person aspect of our relationship suffered. It was not present any more. We forgot how to be friends. As her visits to Ashland increased, we talked less and made love more. Inevitably, this was to be the reason Caren and I would go our separate ways. She wanted more than I could give her. She desired to be my everything. The relationship worsened. Caren's visits became love making sessions...no talking, no laughing, no friendship. What a wakeup call it was for me as our love making turned into sex. But why was this bothering me? Any man in college would have loved to be in my position. Could it have been that I had discovered morals? Was having morals more important to me than having all the sex I wanted? Was my spirit man disappointed and offended by my actions. I'd discover what it was to have a conscience.

Chapter 19
LAST YEAR

Senior year was both exciting and sad. Not a day went past that I didn't think, "Wow, this is it, my last year in college!" I chuckle when I think about how every time that thought came to mind, I'd quickly find a table or wall to knock on. It seemed like bad luck to talk about finishing college. It didn't feel real. Was it possible that after all the hell I went through, I would be fortunate enough to end up a college graduate? For the sake of calling off the evil spirits, I'd always manage to knock on wood. It seemed like the right thing to do.

The roommate thing went okay for the most part. I wanted to make it work. Flea was different from my other two roommates. In our room, he was fun to be around. He joked, talked, laughed, and we enjoyed each other's company. Outside our room, it was totally the flip side. I'd bump into Flea in the cafeteria where he acted like he didn't know who I was. Most of the times, Flea was with his football friends when he'd act like I didn't exist. At first it bothered me since it made me feel as if I embarrassed him around *his* friends.

Maybe it had to do with me being in the theater. The theater world, although it contained notoriety and popularity, drew negative impressions with its alternate lifestyles and unique ways of living.

At Ashland, as I assume in all colleges and universities, the theater majors dressed and carried themselves differently from the general population. Although I carried myself the same all the time, I was still a theater major. I was convinced Flea was unable to deal with the fact that if his friends discovered I was a theater major, they'd rag and tease him to death. Whatever his problem was (because it was *his* problem), I dealt with it by labeling it as an immature act of a freshman. For Flea, it probably was a "guy" thing as well as an image thing. Nevertheless, I liked our friendship when we were alone. And yes, I do admit his not acknowledging our friendship around his buddies hurt.

Flea's behavior reminded me of how I used to be during the school day at Willson; hard, mean, macho, mack, B-boy down, talking and walking to fit the crowd and the company. In our room, Flea was humorous, jolly, conversable, and enjoyable. I realized and accepted all men go through this "Front Up, Front Down" syndrome. Around his friends and football team, Flea possessed a Front Up. Around family and me, he was Front Down. I expressed to Flea I understood his treatment of me around his friends. I informed him I too went through a Front Up - Front Down phase where impressing people was important. I also let him know having gone through the phase cost me. At times, it cost me the loss of a true friend, or the relationship I could have had with someone who cared a lot about me. I wanted Flea to understand what I was trying to say; unfortunately, he never did. In the end, Flea lost me as a friend. It became too difficult to deal with his Front Up. There was so much I could take. After his friendship began to feel hypocritical, I had no choice but to leave the room. I was too close to graduation. I did not need the drama.

As a teacher (and here I go getting technical)... I see the Front Up syndrome on a daily basis. As an educator who brings his work (students) home with him, I am also fortunate to experience the Front Down of students. Though difficult to accept, I have come to understand that children, mostly young men, need to have their Front Up not as a "show off" display, but more as a survival mechanism. Now that I look back at the friendship Flea and I had, I wish I could have simply seen through the Front Up side of him. I would have been able to accept the hurt during the moments of feeling betrayed by him.

I am a firm believer of fate. I think having gone through this experience with Flea, and how he made me feel as his roommate, has come to help me in my everyday job to better understand why my students act the way they do, and why they do the things they do. Once again, I was reminded how God had a reason for my hurt and pain while rooming with Flea.

Besides the social portion of senior year, and dealing with emotions of fear and anxiety, my year went by fairly smooth.

My final performances in the theater included the lead "Charlie Fox" in Speed the Plow and the "Leading Player" in the musical Pippin. Ironically, Flea offered to help work the properties (props) in Pippin. I think it was then when he realized that theater wasn't so bad after all. Nevertheless he continued to act like a complete stranger toward me around his friends.

Caren continued to visit. She saw both shows as well as a few home volleyball matches in which I played. I looked forward to Caren's visits. I savored the moments like walking in the cafeteria with her by my side as Flea and all his friends watched. It put a damper on their constant teasing of him. Caren was no average Latina. She was very meticulous about her appearance in public. She looked like a million bucks wherever she went. Even if it was to a football game, Caren always looked "fine." To the fellas, Caren was "all that and a bag of chips."

Spring semester went by in the blink of an eye. As graduation approached, academics became more intense. My goal was to finish the semester and do my student teaching at home in Cleveland. During the Christmas break, I visited CSA. I asked the principal if it would be okay for me to come in the fall and do my student teaching under Mr. Fisher. I was happy when he replied it would not be a problem. Little did I know, my old friend had a hidden agenda. As I later discovered, the idea of student teaching at CSA had not been okay with him.

Upon returning from Christmas break, the College of Education asked me to make a decision about student teaching in the fall of 1992. I informed them of my meeting with the principal of CSA and expressed he was okay with the idea. The college had assured me they would contact CSA and handle all the paper work.

A month later, the office of education called me to express his regret. CSA's principal had declined my student teaching placement. I was dazed! Although disappointed and a little angry, I had a feeling deep down inside it was too good to be true. I guess it was the principal's way of getting back at me for all the headaches I caused while a high school student. I didn't allow this short disappointment to mar my last semester at Ashland. I continued to search for a school in Cleveland to complete my certification for teaching.

Theater was still a big part my last semester. Although I did not do any acting in the spring, I directed the play, <u>And miss Reardon Drinks A Little</u>. The year before, I chose a scene from this play for one of my directing classes. Doing the entire play was a real experience. It was my shot at demonstrating my directing skills to the department and University. The cast was made up of, for the most part, non-theater majors who showed up to audition. The show was a huge success. Word got around about the fabulous acting and the humor of the show. The play was sold out both evenings it showed.

    The flip side of the show was the pink eye I contracted in the process. A case of the pink eye so bad, it had me to the point of a near breakdown. I was three weeks from finals and could not see or read a thing from the redness, swelling, and the puss in my right eye. The doctors, ointments, eye drops, hot/cold compressions, didn't work....nothing worked! The right eye infected the left eye, virtually making me blind. My eyes became so bad I was confined to my room. There I cried in horror as I thought, "I knew it was too good to be true." How would I take my finals if I could not see or read a thing? I couldn't eat from the depression which took over my life. I wanted to die! I was miserable, frustrated, angry, and very depressed about my eyes. I imagine for Flea, I was unbearable to live with as my mood swings and attitude drastically went from enthusiastic and excited to extremely negative and depressing. It was by the grace of God and divine intervention that I got through finals week.

Over!

College graduation was in my grasp. I was so close I could taste it! There aren't words to describe how it felt to be the only known Latino to graduate from Ashland. The work, the disappointments, the hurdles, the obstacles, the good people, the bad people, the discriminatory comments and remarks, the outcast feelings, the roommates, the name calling, the labeling, the theater students, the Math and English professors, the semester in Spain, the cheerleaders, Flea and the pink eye could not have seemed more trivial. It was over. All of the good stuff and all of the misery was over! In a million years, I never thought, especially after my horrifying middle school and high school experiences, that I would ever see the moment where I would walk across a stage and be handed not one but two Cum Laude college degrees; A Bachelor of Arts in Theater, and a Bachelor of Science in Education. At Ashland, a predominantly white institution, William "Spanky" Mon T. came, sought, conquered, and departed a college graduate! To him I give the highest praise……...HALLELUYAH!

Chapter 20
STUDENT TEACHING

My main concern after graduation was finishing my requirements for teaching certification. The other concern was money for the summer. I needed a job.

When an opportunity arose for me to work at Cedar Point, I took it. Cedar Point is an amusement park in Sandusky, Ohio about sixty miles west of Cleveland. I was happy. It was a sure job. For Caren, it was the start of our finish. She had been anticipating my return from college. She wanted to be near me. When she found out about the job at the Point, she became very angry. She thought I should have consulted with her first before agreeing to take the job. Cedar Point meant moving to Sandusky for the summer. She did not like the idea one bit. Caren threatened to break up with me if I took the job. Although I ended up at the Point, we didn't break, up but our relationship was never the same.

On one of my visits home, I learned about an audition for actors. The zoo was looking for actors to work a summer program. The program, geared to informing zoo guests about the animals through acting, was looking for actors to play the roles of The International Farmer, The African Ranger, The Bird Watcher, The Marine Biologist and the Northern Animal Tracker. The zoo devised this program as a way to guide and educate guests with actors pretending to be these people.

Leaving the Point was not difficult. Although I was having a good time, I missed Caren, my family, J-man and Father D. I was blessed to have found the article about the job at the zoo. I auditioned for the job.

You don't have to be a genius to know who I was hired to play. Being the International Farmer was phenomenal! The exposure I experienced with the animals and reptiles will forever be dear to me. The most exciting part of the summer was the morning talk show I appeared on. Being on television was a lifelong dream come true. The other portion of the summer was the huge article and pictures in the newspaper of me in my costume as I held Roberta, a Rainbow Boa Constrictor.

One day that summer, a friend invited me to a volleyball practice at her old high school. She introduced me to the volleyball coach who was desperately looking for help with her high school team. Since I love the sport so much, I had no problem offering to help on my days off from the zoo.

After the zoo job, I asked the coach if she could talk to the principal about doing my student teaching at the high school. It was perfect. I could do my student teaching and be the assistant volleyball coach. After getting the okay from the principal, I was elated and overjoyed when the coach expressed how happy she would be leaving the team to me the following year. The coach was going to retire. To top things off, one of the teachers in the foreign language department was also retiring.

There was a good chance I could be hired as the Spanish teacher the following fall of 1993. It was a dream come true. I would be teaching high school Spanish and coaching my favorite sport, volleyball.

During summer practice, word got around the high school about the "new" coach. The girls on the team seemed to love the new coach in town. Practices were different for them, more enjoyable, more satisfying, more structured, and more educating. The thirst to win was brought back to Collinwood High School. Since the head coach was leaving to become an administrator, I was running most of the practices, and scrimmages, until our opening match.

I noticed a young lady, whom I only saw once the entire practice season, wearing a uniform. When I questioned where she had received a uniform, she answered, "From coach." When I asked what the deal was, she responded, "I'm a senior." I had surmised she thought that because she was a senior, she didn't see a need to come to practice all summer. I chuckled as I informed her there was no way she would play without having come to practice a single day. The young girl turned her back to me as she sat in the stands and blurted out, "We'll see about that!"

When the coach arrived (just moments before the match), the young girl turned on the water works. She folded her arms as tears poured down her face. After pulling her to the side, the coach came to the scorer's table where she asked for the lineup sheet.

After a quick review of my line up, she balled it up and threw it in the bleachers. From the looks of it, a new line up was made with the addition of the senior girl. Feeling slighted and undermined, I quietly left the stands and went home. There was no way I was going to deal with the "She's a senior, this is her last year..." conversation. I was so angry and hurt, I became disinterested. My only thought as I sat in my living room staring at a blank T.V. screen was, "Why can't things ever go my way just once?" During the following weeks, the girls from the team visited my room imploring me to come back. I just couldn't. I didn't know how to approach the coach about what happened. I was so hurt and felt so bad. That season the girls' only victories were the only four wins I coached during the preseason.

During my student teaching, I learned so much about my

work and my students. The children were challenging, tough, and yet rewarding.

Because I was familiar with the inner-city, the lingo, expressions, mannerisms, music, issues and lifestyles, I had little problems with challenging students. I lived their experience all my life; I could relate. I knew where they were coming from. It all was very familiar to me. In the four months I student taught, I managed to turn around a few hall roamers and drug dealers and get them back into the classroom. The students enjoyed my class. It seemed as if I was teaching at a level that no other teacher could understand. It was neat being talked about in a good way.

Teachers would come up and ask how I could get the students to be so controlled.

I had heard around the building that teachers were stating I was going to be a great teacher. I realized being great meant being in control. I don't remember not being in control during my student teaching. I didn't know having control was such a huge issue in the profession. This was one of those "things" they don't tell you in college. In the teacher's lounge, my efforts, accomplishments, and popularity with the kids were brushed off as, "Aw, He's new," "Oh, he just has that first year teacher energy I once had, it'll wear off. Give him a couple of years." While other teachers expressed how it was the closeness in age.

On several occasions, some of the teachers gossiped about one particular student. They shared their horrifying stories concerning the student. When asked if I had the student, I responded, "Mookie? Oh, he does wonderful work for me. No problem." Mookie was the same student whose mother followed him from class to class one day, carrying a two by four under her arm. I never had a problem with the young man. I felt bad as the teachers crucified him. He was one of those students who just needed some attention. Unfortunately, Mookie only got negative attention. I didn't become a popular character when I took up for Mookie that day. I expressed my philosophy about dealing with difficult children like Mookie. I went into my "front up, front down" theory with the teachers. Needless to say, they were not impressed. And I got the feeling like I had offended some.

In a nut shell, I explained how sometimes teachers tend to talk at students as opposed to talking *to* students. Children have a built-in shut off mechanism. The moment they feel any adult is talking at them, they turn off. They don't hear a word the adult is saying. Inner-city, poor, hard, street core children need to be talked to, not talked at. I explained there *is* a difference. Nevertheless, it was one of the moments where I should have kept my educational philosophies to myself. I quickly learned not to side with students when eating lunch in the teacher's lounge. It was because of this experience I began to have lunch in my classroom.

Toward the end of the semester, the principal asked if I could stay on the staff as a building sub. He also asked if I was willing to resurrect the boys' volleyball program in the high school. When I questioned how long it had been since the school had a boys' team, he responded 1988. How coincidental it was. The last year Collinwood had a boys' volleyball team was the last year they played CSA, the year I graduated from high school.

I was fortunate to be in the building on a daily basis as a substitute. It allowed me the opportunity to recruit boys for the team while earning a somewhat steady income. I had successfully completed student teaching in December, 1992. I remained in Cleveland as a substitute. Most of my assignments were at Collinwood.

As for volleyball, I ran into the same problems from high school as far as practice time in the gym, equipment and uniforms were concerned. I managed to work out a deal with the middle school down the road for a place to practice. I bought most of the equipment, while the boys sold candy to pay for uniforms. My compensation for all that I went through were the guys on the team. The gentlemen, or "my boys," as I referred to them, were a coach's dream. We ended our first season one game above five hundred. And what an inaugural season it became. I wasn't at all prepared for what took place during the Easter break. One of my freshmen volleyball players was killed!

I was eating Easter supper at a friend's house when I learned of the tragic news about Ronnie on the evening news. Apparently, his mother went to church that Easter morning and dropped Ronnie off at his cousin's house. There, Ronnie and the cousin discovered and played with an uncle's loaded gun. When it went off, it shot Ronnie in the head. They kept him on life support for a couple of hours when his mom decided to take him off. Easter Sunday had never been so sad and tragic. Ashland did not prepare me for this part of teaching. How could any college?

I was devastated. Just that Thursday, I took Ronnie home from practice. As he got out of the car, he reminded me to buy more peanut M&M's. Ronnie and the team were feverishly selling candy to pay for volleyball uniforms and warm ups. His last words to me were, "Just because we're on break doesn't mean you can't come get me."

It seemed like the team lived with me. They were always at my home or in my classroom. On the weekends, I'd take them to the movies, Cedar Point, or to play volleyball at the J.F.K. city recreation center. Those were my boys. How I loved my boys!

When asked to speak at Ronnie's funeral, I felt honored. Ronnie's mom talked about his passion for being a better volleyball player. She stated to the church and to me her appreciation for taking such interest, dedication, and time with her son. It hurt my soul to be told that all Ronnie ever talked about was volleyball, and "Mr. M," his coach. To this day, I drive around with Ronnie's picture in my car. Every Easter, I visit his grave and wonder what if he had only went to church with his mom that Easter morning.

Ronnie's number was retired. And my award for Most Valuable Player every year since his death has been named after him. Ronnie's death serves as a reminder every year, at the awards banquet, of how quickly life can be taken away. It reminds me that I am not in control.

God is.

As teachers from all over came to the funeral and shared in Ronnie's going home to his Father, I was reminded by fellow colleagues how the job of a teacher was not an easy one. Teaching not only meant accepting the challenges, obstacles, difficulties, and rewards of child learning, and discovering their strengths and potentials, it also meant having to sometimes say goodbye forever to a child who aspired to be someone in life. To a child who demonstrated potential. To a child who shared a lifelong dream with you. I'll never forget what one of the teachers whispered in my ear the day of the funeral. She said, "Mon T, this is a part of inner city teaching. This was your first and certainly not your last. You will be okay. Give yourself some time."

Will I ever be able to handle another loss such as Ronnie? Some say I get too involved with the students. Others say I shouldn't bring my work home with me. Others who know the good I'm doing encourage me to remain a part of their lives outside of school. Others implore me to continue being a child's guide for success.

As a teacher who continues to bring his "work" home with him, I live each day knowing that I put myself more at risk by opening my personal life to my kids. But my life is incomplete any other way. My kids *are* my life. To know that I make a difference in their world is the pinnacle of any reward a person can achieve. Maybe one day, I will, with no choice, have to relive another "Ronnie" tragedy. It is the chance I have learned to accept and take.

Although I did not remain the head volleyball coach and was not offered the opening in the foreign language department, I remained very close to my high school kids. And was still the boys' volleyball coach despite not getting paid.

After the first season, I was informed there wasn't any money in the school's budget to pay for my coaching stipend. So, I was given a choice: scrap the program and put all my boys out on the street, or coach for free. I elected to coach for free; my boys were worth it. There was no way I would give up. Those boys needed to be a part of something. This team was keeping them off the streets, into their book work, and ALIVE!

My Collinwood experience taught me a great deal about the life of my kids. It has been an experience which I will always treasure.

Sharing in the lives of my inner city children has allowed me to take a closer look at the life I have chosen to live. The life of an educator, friend, confidant, mentor, and sometimes dad. A life that will never make me rich or famous, but will enable me to rest easily at night knowing I have discovered the role I was put on earth to play. The role of Coach and sometimes dad, big brother, uncle, priest and teacher. I had discovered the purpose God had for me. It was a blessing to realize that HE had made my occupation my vocation. I was charged and had to be prepared as I knew full well after Ronnie's death that to whom much is given, much is required!

Chapter 21
ALPHA

My goals up to this point in my life had all been realized. I had managed to achieve what I set out to accomplish except for one aspiration I had always desired; to be a member of the greatest and oldest fraternity of color; Alpha Phi Alpha Fraternity Inc..

My involvement with the minority club in college included the attempt to form Ashland's only fraternity of color. Although it never happened while I was a student, I helped trigger the idea of establishing Ashland's chapter of the Black and Old Gold.

It was during the lateral portion of senior year at CSA that I became interested in Alpha. On a weekend senior trip to Ohio State, I was hosted by a Latino who was a member of the fraternity. He and his roommate (who was also a member) took me to an Alpha function the fraternity held that weekend. That weekend I learned what "stepping and strolling" was and enjoyed the Founder's Day Jam that Kappa Chapter of Alpha through during my weekend visit. I learned a little of the fraternity's legacy of famous Brothers such as Dr. Martin Luther King, W.E.B. Dubois and Thurgood Marshal. And although there wasn't too much information about the fraternity history told to me, I was able to read some Alpha history through a book given to me that weekend. The Latino brother inspired me to read through the book and return it to him upon my freshman year to Ohio State. Since I decided not to attend Ohio State the following year, I never saw or heard from him again. I did manage, however, to educate myself about the fraternity.

It wasn't until Junior year at Ashland that I learned more in depth about the fraternity and the things they do both in college and the community. I was curious, so I decided to inquire about Alpha. My attempts to educate myself about fraternity life and how the world views fraternities proved to be interesting research. Nevertheless, the mere suggestion that a yellow brother like myself, a Colombiano, with no known African roots would try to pledge a predominantly "Black" fraternity did not go over very smoothly with my white counterparts as well as some of my black counterparts. When asked why a black fraternity and told, "You aren't black," I was stumped for an answer. I began to review the real reasons why I wanted to become a member of a fraternity, white or black, period.

I was impressed with Alpha's vision of education and the good things they do for young men. The fraternity's "Go to High

School-Go to College" and "BRICK" programs were programs I could launch after landing a teaching position (I thought). I knew that if given a choice between a white fraternity or a black one, I would feel more accepted and at home with my black brothers. It was natural; I had lived around them the majority of my life, gone to school with them and have even lived with them. Blacks and Latinos have always coexisted since we share more commonalities than differences. Commonalities which include cast typed, slavery, discrimination, stereotyped and racism.

After graduation, I thought my chances of being an Alpha were over. The attempts to form a chapter at Ashland fell short. Time had run out. I would graduate and not have finished the process I had helped to begin. At the time, I was not aware that I could become a member even though I was no longer a college student. It was at Collinwood I discovered my chances and hopes were not dashed. I discovered that black fraternities, unlike their white counterparts, have graduate chapters for men seeking membership. I also learned that the backbones of all black fraternities and sororities are due in great part to the continuing support of its college graduate financial members.

It took a great deal of effort, time, money, and dedication to finally achieve my dream of becoming an Alpha. Its prestige as well as its legacy have played a significant role in my life as I continue to marvel at the fraternity's secrets and hidden blessings. I am amazed when I wear my Greek letters how I end up meeting brothers from all over. Brothers have walked up to me at the malls, clubs, even the grocery stores to greet me with the fraternity grip or by salutations that only we know how to respond to.

It seemed like my goals in life were complete as I walked out of the darkness and into the oasis of Alpha Phi Alpha on June 27, 1993 at 8:17 P.M. The date which proved to be so momentous. It was also the same day that Caren could no longer tolerate my job, my kids, my volleyball team, my fraternity pledging, or my fraternity brothers. It was the same date that Caren decided she could no longer be number two or three in my life. It was the day she said goodbye to me forever. Not knowing how to react, it was a great evening with a bitter ending. God sometimes has to remove some things and some people in our lives in order to receive what he has prepared for you. Although it didn't feel good, it was for my good. I said goodbye to Caren forever.

Chapter 22
MY KIDS

For the next three years, I became a Spanish teacher to third, fourth, and fifth grade children at the Foreign Language Magnet School in Cleveland, Ohio. I was fortunate to have pioneered a new program which embarked on teaching Spanish to elementary children as a second language. I was offered the position the spring I was finishing up at Collinwood High School.

I didn't know what to expect. My entire training at Ashland was geared toward high school. I was not at all prepared to teach young children. My desires after graduation were to find a position in a Cleveland inner city high school while coaching the school's volleyball team. That was no longer an option since I had accepted an elementary teaching position. After all, it was a sure job. Substituting was not what I had in mind for another year. I needed a steady income, medical, dental and vision insurance.

I was asked to teach third, fourth, and fifth grade. My coworker taught the kindergarten, first, and second graders. I was fortunate to have landed the position with such a wonderful person. Mrs. Ramirez was wonderful at helping me the first couple of months with lesson plans, ideas, and techniques for teaching Spanish to young kids. She taught me songs, poems, games and many other enjoyable teaching strategies. It was fabulous working with someone who enjoyed my company.

I was grateful, and always thankful to God for giving me such a great job. I enjoyed my work and enjoy going to work. After my first year, I vowed never to return to the high school level.

Although I missed my kids at The Wood, I was in heaven at the elementary school. My kids sang songs, danced, recited poetry, and repeated everything I asked of them in class. With the high school students, it was like pulling teeth to get them to repeat things in Spanish, more or less get them to sing and dance. My background in theater gave me a good foundation for teaching a foreign language. After a couple of lessons, I discovered how to create small skits for the kids to do in Spanish. My high school kids would have looked at me as if I were crazy. The elementary kids loved acting and performing small skits.

Although my dreams of acting and directing were not pursued, I made the best out of my job. I became the actor and the director as my classroom became the stage and my kids the audience. My students pump the blood that flows through my veins. It is because of my love for them that I have continued to enjoy my life as a teacher. My children allow me to relive my childhood. As I watch them grow both intellectually and socially, I am reminded that life's most precious gift is a child. There is nothing like the feeling I get when they run up and hug me every morning. They became my motivation to continue to study and pursue a Master Degree.

I decided to go back to school after my first year of teaching. My goal: a master's degree in administration. I thought, "Señor Mon T., School Principal" had a nice ring to it. I began to aspire to one day lead my own building. A place of my own where my skills, talents, compassion, enthusiasm and spirit, could be transmitted into the minds of children and its educators. At the time it was a corny deep dream. But what the heck. I never thought I would get this far. I took my chances and applied for graduate school. It was God who had gotten me this far. Since I knew he could do exceedingly, abundantly all I could ask or think, I drove myself to Kent State and started the ball moving on faith.

Chapter 23
ACCEPTANCE

I think one of the most difficult things I experienced as a new teacher was not the anxiety I had with teaching but more the cold treatment from certain teachers in the building. I was the new guy that all the kids loved without having been there a month. All the children talked about was Spanish and Spanish class. To some, that was a threat. To others (thank God, to the majority), it was refreshing to have young spirit in the building since our staff was mainly seasoned and majority female.

I discovered, through talking with my students, what makes children not like certain teachers. When I questioned the kids, most of the responses were, "The ones who always tryin'a dog somebody." It was interesting to me how the kids seemed to bring up the same names. Some expressed, "They prejudice" It didn't strike me as odd since these were the teachers that made my life tough my first year in the elementary building.

Because I wondered what the kids meant, I asked for some examples. Many of them expressed how "these" teachers gave preferential treatment to specific students as far as privileges, treats, rewards, praising, and scolding were concerned. Other kids expressed they didn't appreciate being told, "My five year old could write faster than you. My five year old can understand this work."

It made them feel insulted and offended. After a field trip to the zoo one day, the kids told me how they overheard a teacher joke around saying the monkey island exhibit was family to some of the kids at school.

I realized that teachers like these were what make children hate coming to school. Teachers like these are why some children end up dropping out and going to the street life. It's too bad teachers like this are allowed to teach inner city children, or children at all. Too ignorant to know that comments about monkeys and black people are offensive, racial, and dehumanizing to children, Black children in particular. These are the types of teachers who take advantage of their authority and take out their frustrations (prejudices) on children. These are the teachers who forget that although children are young, they too have feelings and emotions.

Being accepted into the profession had been a strenuous journey. It was arduous trying to remain professional at times when I wanted to defend my kids. Sometimes, I couldn't help but to inform them of their ignorance and ignorant comments. Again, there were times when I should have simply stayed quiet, but I could not stand and watch children be offended. The children were scared to express how they felt for fear of retribution all year long. Because I, on several occasions had defended them, well, it didn't make me a popular colleague.

It was difficult but I had learned how to work with the tension and adversity. I had accepted the fact that there would always be that one person to rub me the wrong way.

It had become a battle, and a true struggle, to remain professional, especially when I'd get wind that Spanish Class was being downplayed by certain colleagues. Some felt Spanish class was meaningless, unimportant, trivial, and unnecessary. Some teachers felt it took away time from more important lessons. Dealing with that was hard for me. I began to pray more and more especially in the mornings. Before I did anything I found myself in early morning devotion asking God for strength to remain cool and professional. I didn't want to cause a scene and lose my job. At times, I felt not teaching English, Science, Math, or History made my role as Spanish Teacher inferior.. The evil one was trying to convince me that the work I was doing wasn't important. I prayed a lot my first year. I couldn't feel unimportant. I had invested too much. Despite the enemy's desire to steal, kill, and destroy my joy my first year was a rewarding experience. Although the struggle to instill importance to my title as Spanish teacher became disconcerting, it proved to be my most challenging year as well.

I had to convince myself that teaching a foreign language was just as important as teaching a major subject. I had to validate my position by instilling in my students the importance of learning Spanish. One day, Spanish will be the second language in the United States. I asked my students never to be too proud or too snobby to learn another language. I wanted them to feel proud to live in the greatest country on earth. But I made it clear that English was not the only language to know.

I was proud to tell them how wonderful it felt to be a bilingual Latino-Americano with knowledge of my heritage and language.

How beautiful it was to hear my students speak my native tongue. How stunning the feeling to know that one day, one of them might have my job or the job of an international interpreter. How beautiful it would be, twenty years from now, to discover that one of my students has used what little I have taught them to become successful in life. What a slap in the face it would be to those who thought, said, and did otherwise. I am certain that one day I will be able to see this dream realized. How pleasing it will be!

As far as for my professional experience, I realized that my illusion of teachers was all wrong. You see, I always thought teachers became teachers because they loved children. There was no way I was going to accept that there were teachers who went into education for summers and weekends off! Unfortunately, I discovered that in many cases, this was true. That realization frightened me! I made up my mind to go into my second year with the armor of God and declare unto myself that no weapons formed against me would ever prosper!

Chapter 24
MY HOUSE

At age twenty-four, God allowed me to accomplish a college career, a half a year of subbing, a full year of teaching, and blessed me with my own home. It was not an easy journey. I had decided to look into a home for two reasons; the fight with my parents and the news I received from Father that he was to be transferred to another church the following year.

I moved out of my parent's house the day I discovered I wasn't done with the ordeal concerning the station wagon Mom and my father financed while I was in Spain. I already had a bad taste in my mouth since it was my credit card that bailed them out. A debt which nobody helped me pay back. I was sick to later discover my wages were going to be garnished because of the bank loan my parents took out to finance the wagon.

It turned out that my parents forged my signature on the promissory note when they were told they needed a co-signer for the loan on the wagon. After the wagon was repossessed and sold, there was an unpaid balance. At the time, my father did not have a steady job, and Mom was only working part time. After discovering the co-signer (me) had a job, the bank's collector came after me for the balance due on the loan. My wages were garnished for a little under two thousand dollars. Not only did I end up paying for the three mortgage payments, attorney fees, and credit card interest, after returning from Spain, I ended up paying off the loan on the wagon as well.

It was the last straw for me. I just could not take it anymore! I was so infuriated, so angry, so overwhelmed with hate and despair, that after telling my parents exactly how I felt, I packed my things and left.

Sleeping was impossible some nights. The dream about me killing my father reoccurred weekly since the day I paid the bank to avoid the foreclosure on my parent's house. After discovering the ordeal concerning the garnishment on my wages, the dream happened almost every night of the week.

I moved to the church. Once again, Father was there for me. He offered me the vacant rectory on the south side of the church with the agreement I would take care of the church facilities during functions and church activities. For Father, it was a concern off his mind. He no longer worried about someone breaking into the old rectory, and I had a place to stay. There is no way in a thousand years that I could ever pay him for all he'd done for me. I lived there for a year until Father was transferred to a parish in Chicago.

Buying a house was no easy task. I had to write a thousand letters to the credit bureaus from all over the country to clean my credit report. My parent's wagon had caused credit problems with my credit report. After what seemed to be an eternity, my credit report was finally cleaned, and I was able to get a loan to purchase a home.

I must have looked at ten houses before coming across *my* home. I was so sick of looking at house after house. Too big, too small, didn't like the neighborhood, too expensive, too crummy, needs too much work, I was at the verge of giving up. I was ready to just rent an apartment and be done with it.

It was just before the end of the school day when I received a phone call in the office. It was my real estate lady. She was sitting in her car in the driveway of a house on the south side of Cleveland. "You have to come, you're going to love this one, I promise," she said. All I did was laugh. "You must be crazy if you think I'm going to look at another house. I am through house shopping. Forget it. I'm tired and I'm going home to rest," I told her. After five minutes of imploring me to come to the house, I gave in and agreed to go see the house. When I pulled up in the driveway I thought, "Hmmm." After walking through the front doors, something inside of me rushed through my heart. It was a feeling of content, sureness, and comfort. This was the house I had pictured in my mind. I moved in three months later, two days before Thanksgiving. How appropriate it was. I sure was thankful for my Jesus and the beautiful little home he put in my path.

The day I was handed *my* very own keys to *my* very own house, I closed the front door of the house and fell to my knees. I banged the floor with my fists as I cried tears of joy. The only thing I could recall saying was, "Thank you Jesus, Thank you Jesus, Thank you Jesus for my house." It was a moment of praise, worship, and thanksgiving. It was a moment of happiness as well as disbelief. I had *my own* house. God the Father had truly blessed me with my very own house. Faith was truly a substance of things not seen, evidence of things not heard.

It wasn't until after I moved into my home that the dreams went away. Not completely away, but they weren't like before when I'd wake up almost every night drenched in sweat. I've come to understand that I built up so much inner anger, my body's only way of releasing all the stress I managed to accumulate was to dream that horrible scene between my father and myself.

The day after receiving my keys, when I finally was told everything was okay with the loan and the bank, I went to work with the intentions of talking to my students about my wonderful blessing. I began all my classes by dangling the keys in front of the children and telling them, "Senor Mon T. is only twenty-four years old, and he has his own house. Anyone of you sitting in this room can have anything you want in life. All it takes is a little patience and lots of hard work. The way to achieve your dreams is to keep your head in your books. Stay away from folks you know are trouble and who'll only bring you down. Boys and girls, you can be successful in life. Each one of you has a mind of your own. Use it. "Milk" school for everything it's worth. When you don't like a teacher, or a teacher doesn't like you, treat it as a job. Punch in, do what is asked of you, punch out. It's simple. Keep your head on your shoulders, and I guarantee any one of you could have *your* own home and more when you grow up."

Looking at the facial expressions, I could tell I got through to most of them. It wasn't until the last day when I realized I had made an impression on the kids, well at least one of my kids. One of the boys came up and told me, "I remember what you tole us when you got your house, Señor. I'ma visit you when I get keys to my own house. You just wait." After hugging the young man and wiping the tears from my eyes, I realized that even when you think kids aren't "getting it," they are. I don't think I'm going to be able to handle the day one of my kids comes to visit me and puts into my hands the keys to his/her own house. I will just die from feeling so proud of them. I pray to God that I made a difference to more than just one on that morning when I shared with my students the joy of having my own home. Living and renting apartment to apartment, house to house all my life wasn't nice. We'd never know how long we would stay, or if we'd be able to pay the rent. Being at the mercy of a landlord to repair things was grueling. The most fear was moving into a place that had mice, roaches or other creatures. I witnessed the struggle with Mom and my father to get a home. After the ordeal with the lawsuit, eyes did not see and ears did not hear the idea of ever owning my own house. I was in awe of God's faithfulness and wanted my students to know that if he could find favor in me, He could find favor in anyone!

Chapter 25

A GOOD YEAR?

Having my own house was more than what I imagined it to be. I was now the happy snow shoveler in the winter, the grass mower in the summer, and the leaf raker in the fall. One of the ladies in the parish, who had been like an aunt to me, gave me her old lawn mower as a house warming gift. It was an expense I did not have to worry about. The only problem was learning how to cut grass correctly. It took some time before I got the hang of it. After a few mows, I was a pro. My house warming and Christmas gift from Father, (as if he hadn't given me enough) bless his heart, was a snow blower. That too was a project in itself. Nevertheless, I enjoyed the feeling of doing both chores since it made me feel like a true American home owner. I remember thinking during all three seasons how wonderful my life was going to be cutting grass, raking leaves, and shoveling snow for all eternity. But I didn't worry too much. One of the wonderful benefits of becoming an educator was picking up wonderful "helpers" to help me do such chores. As Father did with me, I could now pay it forward and bless some of my students with a little spending money and teaching them proud work ethic.

I was excited about the new year. I wanted '94 to be a good year. For the most part, it was. My sister Alina was going to be a high school graduate, and I would be starting my graduate studies at Kent State. It was a miracle she had finished high school. Alina almost didn't make it. Two years prior, she had run away from home and joined a street gang.

It was an episode in our family's life where we thought she was finished. It seemed our family storms never stopped. I am discovering now they did affect our ability to have a normal family. I was the sensitive one always expressing my emotions openly, and talking about my feelings. With my sisters they were more reserved, private and never showing signs of distress. It's odd now that I think about it since people tend to think that women are more open with their feelings while men maintain a more reserved attitude. We were the complete opposite. Mom and my father's quarreling and constant battles obviously affected Alina. She sought the love of a family with the gang she joined. It was by the grace of almighty God she came home and finished high school. We almost lost her to the streets and that gang.

I remember the day of her commencement. When I saw her in her cap and gown as she marched in the auditorium with her classmates, I broke down. All I could do was scream, yell, and holler her name. It was a true phenomenon. I was so proud and so absolutely relieved! I was also proud for Mom. In our community, there were only a handful of mothers that could say all her children graduated from high school. This was an emotional moment for me as I was reminded of all that Mom had sacrificed to come to this country. Giving up her life made it all worthwhile as the youngest of the children was graduating from high school. She felt validated as a mom. I think I was more relieved she had not been killed and that instead of us attending her funeral, we were attending her commencement.

Two months later, Mom, my father, and I took Alina to college in Pennsylvania. It was the start of a good year. But would it finish the same way it had started? I was so used to the evil one lurking about waiting to pounce and devour our joy that I could not help but think that something evil was brewing on the horizon.

Chapter 26
I WAS REALLY THINKING ABOUT IT!

The dreams returned around November of 1994. After taking Alina to college, she returned four months later with news she was pregnant. You cannot imagine how disappointed the family was. It hit Mom very hard.

As a brother, I was more disappointed than anything. I wanted Mom to be able to say she had three college graduates. It would have made her so proud. My eldest sister, although she elected to start a family, completed a business/clerical degree from Sawyer College, I went to Ashland, and the youngest was at LaRouche just beginning her college career in medicine. But to no avail. She came home to have a baby boy. I was to be a new uncle in March of 1995.

I was right back where I had started with the dreams and the endless nights of torture upon discovering what was behind Mom's sudden depression. I had just assumed it was because of

Alina and the pregnancy. But there was more. Right around the end of February after Alina returned home, Mom became withdrawn, mean, and downright sad. Alina's pregnancy was just part of Mom's drastic changes in behavior. She was carrying the worst news of our family's lives.

Mom asked if I could drive her to a doctor's appointment. I had no idea she was seeing a psychologist; no one did.

I found out what had been invading her personality when she returned to the car in tears. Her facial expression looked as though she was in grave despair. She handed me a letter which left me absolutely unconscious.

It had to do with the lawsuit concerning the previous owner of our house. He was back! The letter, in a nutshell, basically stated the house would be auctioned the first week of April. The previous owner and his attorney, almost ten years later, plotted to collect the money my father owed him. The two thousand dollar agreement my father was swindled into signing had, with interest, accumulated to a bill of over twelve thousand dollars! The letter stated that if my parent's didn't come up with the money before April 7, 1995, the house would be auctioned and my parent's, sister, and future nephew would be kicked out on the street.

We tried everything, applying for a third mortgage on the house, going to a money store, refinancing, taking out an equity loan, we even attempted to borrow the money from a friend. There was no hope. The house was lost!

Losing the house caused more pain and suffering in our home. The words exchanged between my father and my mom were dreadful, hurtful, and very painful. It was bad enough as a child growing up with the arguments and fights between the two but now the fighting was vicious and at times volatile. I remember how difficult the moments were when the two exchanged ugly words.

Since in the past my father had twice struck Mom in our presence, there was always the fear that he would hit her again. I used to quail when they'd argue. Living at home was like walking on eggshells or walking through mine fields. You'd never know when some argument was going to explode.

Mom left dad just after Alina was born. By left him, I mean she stopped being his wife emotionally, sexually, and socially. It had gotten so bad that they moved into separate beds and separate rooms.

The worst fights were about the lack of money or my father hitting me, or Mom hitting Gladys. It seemed like when Gladys was punished by Mom, my father would find something to either punish or beat me for. I shrunk when Gladys and Mom fought because I knew later my father would find a reason to kick *my* ass; leaving the T.V. on, leaving a light on, being on the phone too long, not washing a plate, those were just a few of his motivations for beating me. After Alina was born, it seemed like Mom and I were outnumbered. It was always (or it seemed and felt to me) my father and my sisters versus Mom and me.

It all came out in the wash during the waiting period before the inevitable auction of the house. Mom let it all out. She told my father what she thought about him as husband and father. It was not a pretty scene to say the least. She brought up the past, saying things about his drinking, his inability to support the family, his thoughtless decisions concerning the family, and even mentioned his family and the time when she came from Colombia to be his sisters' "esclava" (house slave).

Mom made it quite clear she wanted no more part of my father. She implored him to get out of her life and leave her alone. She denounced the Mon T. name as she vowed never to refer to herself as Mrs. Mon T.

A week after Alina's baby was born, Mom and my father had their last huge fight. The police had to come and escort my father out of the house. At just a week old, the baby, my sister, and my father moved in with Gladys. Mom was left alone in a two-family home. Losing the house was too much for her to bear. She had hit rock bottom. Although no one has ever talked about it, I believe Mom experienced a nervous and mental breakdown.

All logic was completely gone! She had convinced herself that God was not going to allow the previous owner and his attorney to take her home from her. She was positively confident the auction was not going to happen. The frightening thing about the whole ordeal was, she talked about killing the person or people if they came to take her out of the house. She expressed how she would not leave unless they carried her out in a coffin. That was Mom's hard side. The destroyed side of her was her innuendoes about taking a bottle of pills and ending the misery and suffering. The defeated part of her expressed how she would burn the house to the ground before she stood by as someone else took her most precious possession.

From February to the end of March, I had the dream every single night of the week. I woke up sweating, crying, and breathing heavily or not being able to breathe at all.

My heart seemed like it was going to burst through my chest. I couldn't sleep. Teaching was awful. I too, totally changed. I was mean to my students, I didn't feel like giving lessons, I was completely out done and burnt out! Every single moment of the day, every single thought that raced through my mind was the horrid picture of my mom losing the house. I couldn't teach.

I reached the point where anything I consumed I vomited in a matter of minutes. After vomiting blood a couple of times, I stopped eating all together. I went from one hundred eighty five pounds to almost one hundred sixty pounds. I just couldn't eat.

I begged God for my life back. I would have given anything to stop the daily stomach aches, the burning in my throat and chest, the endless and sleepless nights of worrying, and the horrible scenes of Mom losing the house that my mind played over and over again.

I kept looking for the bright side of things but just could not find it.

I kept looking for the lesson to be learned but couldn't see it. I tried to be optimistic but I couldn't. How could anyone? The days and nights got so bad I even contemplated taking my life. I thought, "If I were to die, Mom could have *my* house, and it would be paid for." Could this be a possible solution to all the misery? "Maybe," I thought.

I wanted my joy, peace of mind and happiness to be returned to me. What was I to do? I thought about how Job's wife felt when she demanded, "Curse God and die!" Sometimes, the pain storms come with can take a person to the brinks damning God. All I wanted was to return to my life as I had known it even if it was the life I had before this nightmare.

Dealing with the adversaries in school, with my relationship debacles, dealing with the garnishment of my salary, dealing with the inevitable leaving of Father, dealing with the disillusionment of my sister's pregnancy, dealing with the dream about killing my father, even dealing with being violated, seemed like a bed of rose petals compared to what I was going through.

    Like Job it was a sure test of faith. In the past, I always managed to turn to God when I needed him the most. At this point in the game, I was so angry with him for everything I and the family were going through. "How could a *loving* and *caring* God allow such pain and suffering to happen?", I asked Father. Although, he had no quick answer, he told me that God's ways are not my ways, and God's thoughts are not my thoughts. He said our Lord's plan is not to make his children suffer but to make his children love him more. I realized then, my faith was being tested. Unlike Mom, I had not believed enough in his grace and mercy to understand that everything would be okay. Mom believed everything would turn out okay and it did. She kept speaking God's Word over her life. In Spanish she'd repeat over and over, "I am the head and not the tail. I am above and not beneath. I am blessed in the city and blessed in the field. I am blessed going in and coming out. I am the righteousness of God. I am an heir to the throne of Christ Jesus". Again, Father's words to me were, "When all the doors seem nailed shut, the Lord will open a window."

    As if things weren't already tough, I was secretly agonizing over Father's inevitable departure to Chicago. He announced to the parish he would be leaving July 3, 1995. You can't begin to imagine how horrible it was for me to accept his leaving. Father had been a part of my life since I moved to Cleveland. Although my father was in the home, he wasn't a dad. How would I get through life without him?

He was everything my own father wasn't. Father was my dad. He raised me to be responsible, determined, and optimistic about life. It was because of Father's guidance I had made it through college. It was because of Father I had the will to go on with life when life itself seemed so bleak, horrible, and painful. I could not picture saying goodbye to him. Just the thought of him not being there was so awful. It was more frightening than anything. Up to this point in my life, whenever I was in a jam or needed advice, guidance, or simply someone to talk to, Father was there. I don't know how I dealt with his leaving the parish. It didn't hit me that he was gone until after he left. I kept thinking it wasn't going to happen. It wasn't until about a week after he left that I broke down. God, did I miss him. And still do.

He visited frequently. And even though we had great times when he came home, it wasn't the same. It was another part of life I didn't like accepting...saying goodbye and letting go.

Taking my life seemed like the only way to stop the hurt. On

Easter morning I realized how Jazzy might have felt the day he killed himself. I remember thinking how I could relate to someone having so much pain. In an odd way, I understood why Jazzy did it. Suicide seemed like the only way to relieve all of the anguish, grief and daily torment.

The house was to be auctioned on Wednesday after Easter. Mom and Omari's lawyer had to appear before the judge that Monday if we wished to motion for more time to come up with the money to pay off the twelve thousand dollars. The judge was about to turn down the request and proceed with the auction that Wednesday when Mom blurted out how unjust this was especially when her wages were garnished while she worked at the May Company to pay this debt off.

The previous owner's lawyer had attempted to make it seem like Mom and my father had done nothing to at least try and pay the debt. He wanted the judge to think my parents were simply being uncooperative and unresponsive about the debt all these years.

Mom explained that my father was making payments before his horrific accident and after the accident she continued to make payments through garnishment. The judge motioned for a thirty day continuance. He wanted to investigate and confirm Mom's story about her wages.

The judge gave my parents thirty days and thirty days was all I ended up needing. Omari was back into the picture the day Mom called him for help. I never knew Mom had Omari's number. It was a shock for me to find he and his lawyer were the one's helping and defending my mom. After he left CSA, went to Adams High, and joined the Marines, he came home, got married and started his family. Since the summer of 1988 I had only seen Omari briefly a couple months prior to discovering the nightmare about the house.

That May, we saw each other at Chris's funeral. Chris was a mutual friend of ours. I met Chris through Omari as a sophomore in high school. The three of us hung out together in 87 and 88. We were a trio for two years, calling ourselves cousins. Chris was murdered on the street as someone attempted to steal his friend's Jeep which Chris had borrowed to drive that day. The man, wanting the Jeep for the Dayton wheel rims, shot Chris in the heart, stole the Jeep, and left Chris to bleed to death on the pavement. It was at Chris's funeral when I last saw Omari.

Since I was on a very much needed Spring break from teaching I took the opportunity to ask around for help and advice about the money my parents needed to save the house. I only had thirty days to come up with a plan to avoid the auction. I decided to call my real estate lady. She offered me a number of a friend of hers who worked at a bank. He was a mortgage loan officer. After explaining the ordeal about the house, lawsuit, and what would happen if I didn't come up with the money, he offered me what was to be the grand solution. It was the beginning of the end of what was up to this point in my twenty five years of life, the worst, most horrible four months I had ever experienced.

All the praying I had done to God caught his attention. God listened to my agony, and once again the Blessed Mother Mary had interceded for me. It seemed like all the Rosaries and prayers I had prayed were answered. In a time of desolation, I had not (although I was so close, so very close) lost my faith in God. Although excruciatingly difficult, I believed he would never leave nor forsake me and asked him to forgive my moments of unbelief. Once again, I had turned to a providing God, for help, and he showed up and showed out.

With the pending lawsuit, and the first and second mortgages, already on the house the total debt on the property was right around twenty one thousand dollars. Since Mom's house was appraised at sixty five thousand dollars, she was able to sign over a down payment in the form of home equity, for forty four thousand dollars. In essence, I was able to take out a sixty five thousand dollar mortgage loan to buy Mom's house. The bank applied the forty four thousand dollar home equity as a down payment, leaving a twenty one thousand dollar balance. The bank handled paying the lawsuit, and both mortgages and I ended up with a second home. The mortgage payments of less than two hundred eighty dollars a month were now my responsibility for the next decade. And although I was beyond happy, I could not help but feel very afraid. How was I going to manage two mortgage payments on a teacher's salary? Needless to say, I was terrified. But for the time being, I was more relieved. I had just hoped that maybe Mom would get better, and that she would turn back into the mom I knew her to be.

Based on past experiences, I knew I would be the only one worried about how I would manage. Up to this point, my father, and my sisters were unemployed. The three whom no longer lived in the house, would have nothing to do with helping me out as far as the new mortgage payments were concerned. The only way to be sure I could pay the monthly payments was to rent the upstairs apartment. But Mom was not having it! She refused the idea. She had been through so much. She wanted nothing to do with anybody. She made it very clear she wanted to be left alone! Having tenants were out of the equation. You can only imagine my frustration. Mom downstairs, an empty apartment upstairs; how could I get her to change her mind and help me out some?

The stress the lawsuit caused her completely affected all logic. There was no way she could live on the fixed income she now received from the government and pay the new mortgage. I didn't want to see her struggle to make ends meet. During the week I was at the bank, she promised me she would rent the upstairs once the house was out of jeopardy of being lost.. When the problem was fixed, she had forgotten about our agreement to rent the upstairs apartment. There was always an excuse. She claimed there were too many repairs to be done. She'd say the apartment was not up to code and needed too much work before it could be rented

The upstairs sink needed to be replaced so I bought a new one, and replaced it myself. The bathroom needed a shower, "No one likes a tub without a shower." she said so I bought the tub a shower adaptation, and installed it myself. She stated the ceiling in the bathroom needed to be scraped and painted so after scraping and painting it, she mentioned the walls, the doors, and the floors needed to be repaired. It became one thing after another, excuses and reason why the apartment could not be rented.

For the first time in my life, I was irritated and angry with Mom. My concern was the new house payment. I was deathly worried I would get put in a situation where I would not only lose Mom's home but my new home as well. Even though Mom was opposed, I decided to go ahead and put an ad in the paper. My plan was to interview prospective renters and select the one I thought would be most appropriate. Mom threatened if I attempted to put someone over her head to make her life more miserable, more than it already was, she would go to the basement and cut off all the water and electricity to the upstairs apartment. It was after this threat that I stopped talking to Mom for months. I was to the point where I did not care if she was going to struggle to survive. I told her I didn't care what happened. I informed her if she so much as missed a payment, I would put the house up for sale and that would be the end of it!

I don't know how she had managed, but she made all of the house payments during the time I stopped speaking to her. Although I acted like I didn't care, I did. I constantly worried about Mom's ability to pay the light and gas bills. I decided to start sending her fifty dollars a month. At first, I wrapped the money in notebook paper and sent it to her anonymously; later, when we began communicating again, I started sending her a monthly check.

This episode in my life was the reason for writing this journal of memories. Maybe being able to write has allowed me the chance to vent. I was cheated out of a normal life. It wasn't fair to me that I had to be the one carrying this burden. What a price for doing the right thing with my life. My God, was this the beginning of what my life would be like?

I wanted to share how I made it through yet another crisis. Up to this point I never thought twice about my trials and tribulations. I always thought I was going through what any other normal person goes through. It wasn't until after all the affliction I went through with the house that I realized all this was not supposed to happen to a normal person. My woes and tragedies are not meant to come off as something grandiose. Something that was life threatening. I know good and well someone out there is going through much worse. But it was a lot to carry mentally. That pulsating thumping in the base of my neck and the burning in my gut was my bottling all these emotions. Keeping these stories private was only tearing me up inside. I had to let them out before I gave myself a stroke.

My furthest intention is to make anyone think I am boasting about being a strong person. In fact, for many years, I considered myself a punk. The evil one tried to convince me I was defeated. He unsuccessfully tried to kill my spirit and my faith. I know it was his demons that continued to invade my thoughts for many years.

Revealing my thoughts and exposing myself to this pain again was to risk unlocking unhappy episodes that I managed to bottle up and keep hidden all these years. It has taken years and years to release these private plights. Will I inspire someone who is going through some hell in their life to go on, no matter how screwed up things may seem? I hope. Will I give someone the courage to push their way through? Pray their way through? Praise their way through? I believe that I receive someone will! IN JESUS NAME!

Chapter 27
THE END OF THE FIRST QUARTER

The end of my first twenty five years came to a close just as it began. With more attacks from the evil one; drama, drama, and more drama. Jerome moved in with me when he turned fourteen. He was no longer my little J-man. He was now a young man. He moved in because his mother could no longer deal with him. Jerome had completely changed his behavior, attitude, and respect for himself as well as others in his life. Enter marijuana, weed, chronic.

Through Mr. Steinmetz, I discovered Jerome was doing horrible at CSA. He was failing, cutting class, and had started to hang around the wrong crowd. It wasn't until later when I discovered Jerome had been suspended for smoking marijuana.

At first, I hoped it was an experimental thing with him. I tried convincing myself he was a teenager going through normal teenage stuff. "When he figures weed will ruin his life and his relationship with me, he'll let it go," I prayed. Tragically, it didn't happen. So, I sat down with him. Gave him the run down about weed, and all the "Don't do drugs," speech.

I felt good about our talk. He seemed sincere. "It was just a couple of times. I don't do it all the time. I will never do it again." I believed it. I believed him. How could I not? He was my boy. I was his Godfather. He had never disappointed me before. In fact, any problem we had in the past was dealt with. Every problem we shared at this point in our lives, had a solution. A solution that allowed us both to move forward.

Jerome promised he'd never do it again. Until one evening when he showed up at my front steps with all his belongings. It was then I had to accept he had a drug problem. It was either let him stay with me, or he was on his way to juvenile detention. This was the same little quiet boy I fell in love with just four years ago. It didn't seem real. My heart began to get cold. I felt that squeamish feeling in my gut, the kind that makes you sick to your stomach. Shattered and hurt all over, I opened the doors to my home and allowed Jerome to enter. I thought, "Okay God, if this is what you want me to do, I'll accept the challenge." I took him in hoping I could talk some sense to him. But I couldn't.

Jerome thought he was invincible! His thoughts and perception of life were so simple. "You only have one life, one childhood. Why not enjoy it? I ain't addicted. I just be smoking once in a while," he informed me. Smoking marijuana became his life. To him, a party, a dance, even the skating rink, or hanging out with his friends, were no fun or complete unless he had a hit. There was no changing his mind. I had discovered there was cunning, and slick side of Jerome and it destroyed me. Is this what Mom and my father felt when Alina left home and joined a gang? I had experienced my first pain as a parent of sorts.

I caught him in lies about his whereabouts and who he was with. Sometimes, he'd come home after school looking dazed, and acting sluggish. He had been with his boys getting high.

I realized I had lost my Godson to marijuana. The worst part was losing the trust I had in him. Jerome made me realize another aspect about parenting. Is this how Mom felt every time she caught us in a lie or doing something that disappointed her as a mother? Ringing in my ears was her Spanish accent, "Wait on til jew have cheeldren den you weel see." She warned us that one day when we became parents we would understand the pain of a parent.

I considered J-man my son. When he needed shoes, a haircut, clothes, or simply wanted spending money for skating or the movies, I provided him with it. It was no big thing. I enjoyed the feeling of being his Godfather, although to me he was more like my own son. When I saw how he had changed, I was crushed. The street life had taken him over. The way he talked and wore his clothes were signs that he wanted to live the thug life. It wasn't long before it had taken him over completely. He no longer talked in complete or grammatically correct sentences. The street jargon had completely engulfed his entire vocabulary. His clothes were three times his size, especially his pants, "saggin," worn almost down to his knees exposing half his buttocks. This was to be Jerome's new way of life. It didn't make any sense whatsoever. How could this happen? What caused it? I asked God to Please Help!

Jerome was an intelligent and talented young brother. There was no need for him to act like a "nigga" off the street. "Nigga," the word the he and most young brothers (and in some cases, sisters) used in place of friend, homeboy, partner, someone you are cool with, a buddy, a pal. Nigga, a person (regardless of color) who has no morals, scruples, values, dignity or self-respect.

During his brief stay with me, Jerome's mother enrolled him into a detoxification program at the St. Alexis Hospital. Jerome was livid. He could not understand why. He was in denial about his drug addiction, saying we were blowing it out of proportion. He could not see that he was failing school and becoming addicted to pot. After talking to the detox counselor, I realized my J-man was gone forever. The counselor suggested Jerome might start stealing to acquire money for his addiction. He convinced me Jerome was a true actor and a professional, especially when it came to playing with my feelings and emotions for him. He put the fear of God in me when he told me that in the past he has worked with kids who have waited for their parent's to go to work for them to break in and steal their belongings for drug money. This was my biggest fear since Jerome knew I would be teaching.

I wasn't going to give up on him I refused to believe that God couldn't fix this. God could do anything but fail. I loved him enough to give him the benefit of a doubt. I promised to stick it out as long as he promised to get detoxed. He did, so I did.

Unfortunately, after a couple of months and realizing he would not change his behavior, I returned him to his mother. It drove a knife into my heart to cut myself off from him. I stopped calling and picking him up. For almost half a year. "Tough Love," they said. "You're his only lifeline. You have to stop enabling him and show him tough love." It was tough. Tough for me to take him home. I felt like I had failed him. How could Jerome choose weed over me? How? It hurt not being able to call or see him. I wanted him to realize he had lost an important person in his life. I wanted him to stop smoking. It was the only way I would come back.

Going back to school was the best thing that could have ever happened. It kept me occupied and my mind off of how badly I really felt about Jerome. I continued to pray for him every night.

Since God had blessed me with so many miracles, I asked him to help Jerome. The only part that made me sad was knowing the miracle would not come true if Jerome did not want to help himself. He was convinced there was no need for all the intervention. Jerome was convinced he was free from danger. It never crossed his mind that his smoking could lead him to crack, cocaine, or other more worse drugs. He was confident it was never going to happen to him. I recalled asking him what if he got a hold of some bad stuff and smoked it? With that superman attitude, he responded, "It ain't gonna happen cuz I only be smoking wit my friends." Jerome convinced himself he was omnipotent from all danger.

Going back to school would help me financially. I would move into a higher pay bracket and if I landed an assistant principal position I would make considerably more. Being in school also allowed me the opportunity to defer all the loans from Ashland. Deferring twelve thousand two hundred dollars sounded okay with me considering my finances were tight with two mortgages and two homes to maintain!

It was difficult teaching and going to school. Driving an hour to and from Kent once a week was torture. But it had to be done. Alphadom had a lot to do with my decision to pursue a Master's Degree. All those professional men in my fraternity. It made me work harder to move on up and get a piece of my own pie. I decided to attend Kent because of the good reputation of their College of Education. However, I discovered little by little that those rumors were just that, rumors. Kent turned out to be a bad nightmare.

The beginning course work was fairly easy for the most part. I was accepted on probationary basis for having scored poorly on the GRE the Graduate Record Exam. It wasn't a big concern since I had never done well on any standardized tests. And although my scores out of high school on the ACT and SAT were not exemplary, I did fairly well at Ashland.

Kent informed me I had to pass two courses with a B or better to be fully accepted into the graduate program. I talked to several of my classmates and discovered one of those courses had a reputation for being the hardest, in the administration program. Being extra prepared for the Public School Law was my mission. I contacted the professor for advice and suggestions on how to better prepare for this course. He suggested I buy the text book and read it from cover to cover. So I bought the book and did just that. The entire summer of 95, I spent reading school law.

I prepared for what turned out to be the worst class I ever took. What a nightmare the first day of class turned out to be in the fall of 95. The professor informed the class of thirteen, our final grade would be based solely on two scores, a midterm and final exam.

    The professor made me feel uneasy. He had a "mightier than thou" personality and didn't think anything about making you feel just plain stupid. When it came to knowledge of law, the man was brilliant. He spewed every case law possible forward and backward and could regurgitate information from my famous summer reading text, by heart. But as a teacher, he lacked warmth and personality. How could someone in education be so cocky and arrogant toward his students? Although throughout the semester he continued to praise me for answering questions correctly, I always felt an underlying, patronizing, and condescending tone from him. It irritated me. At some points it became offensive. It became so offensive that while everyone laughed at his jokes, I would sit stern faced without much expression. It was my way of saying defiantly, "I don't think jokes at someone else expense is humorous." He became a real problem when he began bashing Ashland. Calling it a water downed version of a university. He'd poke fun at the standards he felt were inferior to those of Kent. Somehow, I felt as if though he had secretly looked over my background and knew I attended Ashland. I began to think he was purposely poking fun of Ashland to irritate me. I was silly for allowing him the pleasure of knowing his comments bothered me.

I loved my alma mater and did not appreciate the ill comments. Although my first year at AU was tough, defending its honor was important. Stating Ashland was "water downed", was saying I was water downed!

I should not have given him the satisfaction and pleasure of seeing my irritation but it was hard to conceal. The thought of giving up my summer to read a five inch thick text book on school law worsened my disdain for this man. It wasn't until the end of the semester that I realized all his praising was all patronizing.

It was difficult for the majority of the class to keep up with all the ridiculous reading assignments as well as dealing with his weekly two hour lectures. He hardly allowed anyone to ask questions or take effective notes. The worst part was asking him to clarify something which was unclear. He made it a point to make you feel as if though you were S.O.S. (stuck on stupid).

After walking out of the midterm, I was so relieved and happy. I felt good about my exam. There was no way I didn't get an A or B. The midterm was twenty pages. It was majority multiple choice with all the answers being correct. The catch was that one was more correct than the others. It was like taking the ACT all over again. For me, it was a personal victory since it was the first test since sophomore year at Ashland that I took in the classroom with the rest of the students.

I had suffered from test anxiety all my life but didn't know it until I identified it as a sophomore in college. I remember how I hated taking assessments. It seemed to me as if everyone was going faster than me. I'd begin to sweat and panic, causing me to draw complete blanks. At Ashland I was allowed to go to a secluded area and take my exams. I was accommodated with extended time and quiet space.

I performed a lot better when I didn't have to hear the shuffling of pages and the sound of pencils and erasers. How I hated taking tests with others around. The sweating, heart beating in my throat, the droplets of water running down the side of my face gave me nausea. I agonized during midterms and finals, feeling like the oxygen was being sucked right out of my lungs. Test taking was just plain painful.

Taking the midterm in the school law class was triumphant for me. I thought I had completely conquered my anxiety. When the professor handed me the exam the following week, I was shocked, sickened, stunned and deeply saddened.

I had ranked thirteen out of thirteen and received a C-. When I reviewed the test in his office after class, I noticed all of my errors were on the last three pages of the exam. The grade I received destroyed my confidence. This meant I needed an almost perfect score on the final in order to earn a B and remain in the graduate program. It was not going to happen. A week after the New Year, I received a letter from the dean informing me I was terminated from the graduate program.

When I called Father in tears, he suggested I fight the dismissal. It was unjust what Kent had done. With the C I earned in the course, I still had a 3.0 grade point average. Under any other circumstances, the college's policy allowed up to seven hours of C work before one could be dismissed from any graduate program. I was being kicked out for those poor GRE scores.

It was unfair that my admission as a graduate student was based only on those scores and no other reason. I had brought two cum laude degrees and a grade point average of 3.5 from Ashland. My letters of recommendation spoke of my abilities and strengths as a teacher as well as a person. How could this happen to me? Was this the beginning of a new storm?

After my first and second appeals were turned down, I began to think that earning my master degree would not come to fruition. I knew I had to do something. Father said to me on the phone, "All things are possible through Christ Jesus. If this dismissal seems impossible to overturn than great, God's specialty is brining to life that which you are convinced is dead".

Before my dismissal, I was one of three non-white students remaining in the education administration program. I wrote the dean a letter hoping she would consider an audience with me.

In my letter, I acknowledged I failed to meet the probationary basis for admission in the program, although I continued to remain steadfast in my belief that students should not be judged on the sole basis of tests like the GRE. I expressed to her that these styles of assessments, in my opinion, were culturally biased and prejudicial to people of color, people like myself. I expressed regret there were no other opportunities to demonstrate my growth, knowledge and comprehension in the course other than two tests all semester.

I wanted her to see me as a person and express to her that as a Latino I have realized the battle to success in this society did not only include those obstacles which the everyday man experiences, but in addition to, are those obstacles which people of color have experienced for many centuries.

Would she understand that my desire to be a principal was not solely for personal gain and benefit but for the people in my life, in my job, and my community? How could I tell her of all the people in my life, especially the kids I taught who have continuously viewed me as a role model, an inspiration, hope, and most importantly, reason to "keep on keeping on" no matter how many obstacles put in one's path? I wanted her to get that it was because of them I have found the will and strength to tolerate professors like the one teaching school law.

As the dean of her college she needed to hear that at the very core of education we should see students as individuals and not judge them only by their test scores. As educators we need to take into account other talents, skills, experiences, characteristics and qualities which students possess and can bring to an institution of learning.

I asked her to reconsider the judgment which had been made in regards to my graduate status. After meeting me in person and hearing about my school law experience she readmitted me into the program in April of 96. I was allowed to continue my studies as a graduate student. It was another victory in my life due to faith and prayer. It was the last battle before my twenty-sixth birthday. Less than a month later, I would be a quarter century old plus a year. I was relieved I could finish the first quarter of my life on a happy note or not?

Two weeks before my twenty-sixth birthday, I received a very exciting phone from the Bone Marrow Society.

The fall of 1993 a few months after my initiation into Alpha, I attended my first regional convention in Louisville, Kentucky. That same weekend of our convention, the bone marrow society happened to be conducting a drive in the same hotel. A representative from the society came to one of our open Alpha meetings and asked the brotherhood to come over to the other ball room and donate blood. I, along with many brothers, in support of the drive gave blood. I felt honored to see the number of fellow Alphas who rolled up their sleeves and donated. It was in the nature and character of the fraternity to step in and support a worthy cause. The brothers who donated blood were informed in the event of a match, someone from the society would contact us immediately.

The woman over the phone asked me if I recalled giving blood at the marrow drive in Louisville. At first I didn't; I had completely forgotten all about it. The representative asked if I would consider reporting to the Red Cross facility in downtown Cleveland because they were certain that they had a nineteen year old man who matched my blood type. She gave me an opportunity to mull the idea and give her a call before the week's end with either decision.

I really didn't need the time she was offering since immediately I knew this was another blessing I was being presented from above. It was my chance to truly pay it forward and bless another life with life. I made an appointment and reported to the Red Cross.

Before beginning the questionnaire the representative explained the bone marrow procedure. She was transparent and very direct about the implications of donating marrow. I learned the procedure would be painful, and it would not guarantee that the patient's body would accept my marrow. There was a chance the marrow could be rejected and the patient could either die or continue to wait on a national donor's list for a match. Should I move forward with the procedure? Was it worth the pain? Yes!

After our brief consultation the representative was pleased that I still had intentions to go ahead and begin the process. She handed me a brief questionnaire with a pencil and informed me it was protocol to ask some last minute questions. Did I smoke? Did I drink? Have I used needles for drugs? Had I had any debilitating diseases like cancer, polio, or diabetes? Had I in the past decade ever engaged in homosexual activities?

Frozen with fear and disbelief she came over and asked if there was a problem. She obviously saw the distraught expression on my face. I couldn't speak right away. I felt my ears and face burn with embarrassment and knew that shame was written all over my face. Numb, stuck and confused I simply pushed the questionnaire toward her and said, "I think I have to say yes to the last question". Just as bewildered as I was, she asked me to explain why I would answer yes.

Before I could speak another word I dashed toward the men's restroom and dry heaved over the sink. I splashed water on my face to clear away the shock, dried off, and went back to the table where she had been waiting with what appeared to be genuine concern. There was no way to get out of marking the "yes" box. She definitely knew that there was something wrong.

Should I lie? Should I just mark the "no" box and make up a story about running into the restroom? Would I be able to live with myself for not being forth right about another person's ability to live or die? Maybe it wouldn't matter. Maybe she would say being raped didn't count as a "yes". Maybe the question was aimed towards individuals who were at risk for contracting HIV? But then why not ask if I was sexually active? Gays and Lesbians were not only at risk, any promiscuous person was at risk of not only contracting HIV and AIDS but other dreaded diseases (this *is* what I was taught. Why this question Jesus? Why here? Why now? Why did the bone marrow society need to know if I had had homosexual sex?

Wrenched and pain filled as it was I began to explain the short version of my attack to a complete stranger. In the middle of what transformed into a sobbing session with her, she oddly allowed me to finish my story, embraced me and stated that it was with great disappointment she had to defer me from being a donor. She offered me a pamphlet with the words "Grief Recovery" written on it and suggested that I go home and consider signing up for the 12 step classes.

I went home and got into my prayer space where only I knew it existed. In front of the self made shrine of our blessed mother and a gold cross that Father gave me before he left, I began hitting my head and pulling my hair. I was angry, upset, saddened by my inability to help a dying teenager, and frustrated that I could not turn back the hands of time and leave the Indians game with Omari. I should have ran or fought like hell to get away. I should have transformed myself into the person in my dream and escaped from those bastards before they penetrated me. I should have fought harder to get away. I pushed the pillow into my face so that I could yell and scream without anyone hearing my cries of agony.

It was two thirty in the morning when I pulled myself up of the floor and crawled into bed. "Thank you Jesus for taking me through this pain now rather than later. Thank you for sparing me the discomfort of the marrow extraction and the sadness of my bone marrow being rejected from this nineteen year old", I thought. This was God's way of letting me he was in control. Although it was very early in the morning I was convinced I heard His voice tell me this and it *did* console me then and consoles me now.

Two weeks later I celebrated my twenty sixth year birthday. I took time to reflect that day on a rock overlooking Lake Erie. As the sun set in the distance I thanked God for the experiences I had lived through and thanked him for loving me so much that he prevented me from doing what the evil one had planted in my thoughts during the lawsuit.

God was preparing me at a young age to live for him. To depend on him for strength and courage. To rely on him for everything. He was teaching me the difference between being in the world but not living in the world. He was calling me to fulfill a purpose he had set out for me when my mom left her life in Colombia with me in her womb. He knew then her sacrifice would not be in vein. Although I pushed to resist him in my early years he led me through storms that only in his grace and mercy I could survive.

I grew up not having much but what I did have was His presence in my life through school at the Mac, through Father, and a praying mother. I used His spirit to create strength in me and continue moving forward and over every obstacle that the evil one placed in my path. The obstacles of a father who really never knew his only son, the challenges of siblings who rivaled me over what appeared to be the love of my mom and the attention of my father, the needs we lived with when it came to financial stability, the alcohol abuse we witnessed, and the rape I endured all created a fighting spirit in me that I never owned or thought I could possess.

I was truly blessed and highly favored in that God had shown me the purpose for my life. The kind of purpose that many seek, and sadly never find because they don't know Him.

As the sun set and the darkness captured the water hitting the rocks, I accepted God's role as provider of my family both for a mom that gave all she could, and siblings that turned to me in the absence of a father that still to this day seeks to find comfort and relief from his own personal demons.

I accepted his gift to be an educator of young minds. And although it may not draw the prestige of a CEO, Lawyer, Physician, or Professional Athlete, I do know with all my heart that my work is being tabulated by a much high authority. I know who is my source and from whom I get my strength. Despite that I have not attained all that I desire to attain, that I don't live where I desire to live, that I don't earn what I would like to earn and that I haven't met the person whom I would like to spend the rest of my life with, In know that he will always provide, never hide, and continue to be a faithful and awesome God. I believe that I receive because I know in my spirit He is not done with me yet.

www.ingramcontent.com/pod-product-compliance
Lightning Source LLC
LaVergne TN
LVHW051225080426
835513LV00016B/1410